CULTIVATING SPIRITUAL FRUIT

Cultivating Spiritual Fruit

ROBERT C. GAGE

Regular Baptist Press
1300 North Meacham Road
Schaumburg, Illinois 60173-4888

Cultivating Spiritual Fruit

Regular Baptist Press, Schaumburg, Illinois
Printed in U.S.A.

Library of Congress Cataloging-in-Publication Data

Gage, Robert C., 1941-
Cultivating spiritual fruit.

Includes bibliographies.
1. Fruit of the Spirit—Biblical teaching.
2. Bible. N.T. Galatians V, 22-23—Criticism, interpretation, etc.
I. Title.
BS2655.S62G33 1986 234'.12 86-20395
ISBN 0-87227-114-5

To my parents, George and Elizabeth Gage, whose consistent Christian lives brought me to personal faith in Christ and continue to provide an example of what it means to walk in the fruit of the Spirit.

Contents

FRUIT OF THE SPIRIT

(Based on Galatians 5:22, 23)

O what a ***love*** Heaven gives to our being
When through the crimson of Calvary's tide
We have been joined to the Church called His Body,
When through the Spirit we're drawn to His side.

O what a ***joy*** in this wondrous salvation,
Not just a sinner who's pardoned and free,
But "one in Christ," heir apparent with Jesus,
He gives His life and His merits to me!

O what a ***peace*** in this Savior abiding,
Heavenly calmness is ours through His cross;
Sin's questions settled, there's rest in the bosom,
Works and self-righteousness counted but dross.

O what ***longsuffering,*** a fruit of the Spirit,
Can be the portion of those who believe,
Taking life's ills from the hand of the Giver,
Sweetly and patiently all things receive.

O for His ***gentleness*** mellow and tender,
As for the wayward and troubled He cared;
Pray be not haughty or forward or stubborn,
Take all the evil, seek not to be spared.

O fill with ***goodness*** my life to o'erflowing,
Make every moment a symphony sweet;
All of the deeds of the flesh so discordant
Brought in subjection and laid at His feet.

O for a ***faith*** that at nothing is daunted,
Strong in the Lord, leaning hard on His Word;
Soon to exchange it for sight more apparent,
There where the song of the angels is heard.

O just a bit of Thy ***meekness*** my Savior,
To be "the least," when of self I would boast;
Finding my glory and strength in Thy favor,
Know in my weakness Thy grace can do most.

O to mix all with a ***temperance*** holy,
Lusts of the flesh now in perfect control;
His to the nth of our innermost being,
Keeping in balance the body and soul.

O in the "fruit" see the portrait of Jesus,
He our example and indwelling Friend,
As we are yielded, He gives us the victory,
Crowned "Overcomers" we'll be at the end.

— Henry G. Bosch

(used by permission)

Foreword

No one would doubt that Satan's primary goal is to keep people from trusting Christ as Savior. The Scripture clearly says, "But if our gospel be hid, it is hid to them that are lost: In whom the god of this world hath blinded the minds of them which believe not, lest the light of the glorious gospel of Christ, who is the image of God, should shine unto them" (2 Cor. 4:3, 4).

If he is not successful in deterring man from responding to the gospel, his next best approach is to confuse mankind on the subject of the Holy Spirit. Just as one cannot be a Christian without *Christ,* so a person cannot be spiritual without a right relationship with the Spirit. It is very important, therefore, that we have a clear understanding of the meaning of the spiritual life.

Dr. Robert Gage has set forth in a clear, remarkable fashion the way a believer can cultivate spiritual fruit. Dr. Gage lays a good foundation by setting forth a Biblical basis in pneumatology in the first chapter, then following it with the secret and evidences of the Spirit-filled life. Then he moves into appropriate explanation and application of the Spirit's work. Having covered the nine aspects of the fruit of the Spirit, the final chapter sums it up appropriately with walking in the Spirit.

While a great deal has been written about the Holy

Spirit, it is difficult to find a book that articulates the subject so simply and clearly as *Cultivating Spiritual Fruit*. We commend it to our reader, praying that the truth of the Spirit will become more than just an intellectual belief. To be spiritually filled daily is the author's final injunction. This book will help and direct you in that quest.

Charles U. Wagner, D.D.

Introduction

To the Christian today, no subject is more important, yet more misunderstood and misapplied, as the ministry of the Holy Spirit. We need as never before to understand not only the doctrinal truth relating to the Third Person of the Trinity but the practical experience of Him in our daily lives.

Some people claim an emotional experience or the exercise of a spiritual gift as proof of the Holy Spirit in their lives. But Jesus said, "By their fruits ye shall know them." Each Christian must examine his own life for the basis of his claim to being a spiritual rather than a carnal person.

After an examination of the doctrine of the Holy Spirit, we shall consider the secret of a Spirit-filled life and the evidence of such a life as seen in the fruit of the Spirit. Each aspect of Spiritual fruit—love, joy, peace, longsuffering, gentleness, goodness, faith, meekness, temperance (self-control)—will be individually examined. We will seek to discover how this Spiritual fruit affects our mental and emotional health, temperament and actions. Our goal is to provide each believer with the means of cultivating spiritual fruit in his life. The result should be the victorious life of the Spirit in the daily life of the believer.

This study does not claim to be the final word on the fruit of the Spirit. In reality, it is a study guide to involve you in the cultivation of spiritual fruit. Each chapter deals with a separate topic related to spiritual fruit bearing. At the close of each chapter you will find a resource bibliography to help you dig deeper into the soil of the subject. The resource bibliography will be followed by suggested discussion questions or projects which are the tools of cultivation. You may labor in the garden of study by yourself or involve others.

Cultivation comes by long, hard work, not quick emotional experiences. It involves breaking the hard soil, destroying the weeds, preserving the moisture and growing the plants. Cultivation means to improve by care, training and study. It is developing growth by constant care and effort. There are no quick, easy answers or procedures. The cultivation of spiritual fruit is a life-long process. If done faithfully here on earth, it will be rewarded in Heaven, when the Master of the vineyard exclaims, "Well done, thou good and faithful servant."

Robert C. Gage

Chapter 1

The Doctrine of the Holy Spirit

J. Edwin Orr has remarked that Charles Finney once looked at a scoffer and the scoffer got saved. Such was the power of the Spirit in a sanctified life. As the Welsh revivalist Evan Roberts would look around the assembly, people would come under conviction of sin, so great was the Spirit's power through a clean channel. If we are to know the power, blessing and fullness of the Spirit, we must first learn Who He is.

I. The Holy Spirit as a Person

At a certain Bible conference, a woman engaged the speaker on the subject of the Holy Spirit. She continually referred to the Holy Spirit as "it." When a little toddler came running across the auditorium and latched fast to the woman's leg, the speaker changed the subject. He asked, "Is it your child? It has pretty hair; its eyes are a beautiful brown. Can it talk? How old is it?" Finally, in exasperation, the woman responded, "Please don't call him, 'it'!" "That's just the point," replied the speaker. "The Holy Spirit is also a Person and should not be called 'it.' "

Many think of the Holy Spirit as a force, an influence or some type of energy flowing from God. In the early centuries of the Church Age, false teaching crept into church doctrine.

At the time of the Reformation, the Socinians denied the deity of the Holy Spirit. Although their false teaching was rejected by the mainstream of Christianity, the church began unconsciously to think and talk of the Spirit as being merely an influence. It is important for us, therefore, to understand the personality of the Holy Spirit.

One proof of the Spirit's personality is the name Jesus gave to Him. In John 14:16 and 16:7 He is called "Comforter," or "one who is called to your side to help." The same word is used of Christ in 1 John 2:1. Jesus said the Comforter would personally guide the disciples just as Christ had done. The Holy Spirit was to take the place of Christ. Only another Person, not a force, could do that. Jesus continually referred to the Holy Spirit by the masculine pronoun "He."

While the authority of Christ is sufficient to prove the deity of the Holy Spirit, there are other proofs from the Scriptures. The Bible shows Him *acting* as a Person. He teaches, testifies and witnesses. He guides, convinces, restrains, commands and directs people. He performs miracles. He calls and sends missionaries into service. He prays for Christians in times of distress and need. These are not actions of an impersonal force but of a Person.

Further proof is seen in the way the actions of others affect Him. The Bible speaks of Him as being resisted, vexed, grieved and blasphemed. In order to be insulted and offended, He must be a Person. One does not blaspheme or grieve an attribute or a force of God. Therefore, it is clear that the Bible ascribes personality to the Holy Spirit. But it goes even further.

II. The Holy Spirit as a Divine Person

As a Person, the Holy Spirit stands in unique relation to Christ and the Father as a member of the Trinity. Several Bible passages show the deity of the Spirit in relationship to the Trinity:

"Go ye therefore, and teach all nations, baptizing

them in the name of the Father, and of the Son, and of the Holy [Spirit]" (Matt. 28:19). Notice that while all three Persons of the Trinity are mentioned, there is the singular "name." They are distinct Persons but one Essence. All are deity.

"The grace of the Lord Jesus Christ, and the love of God, and the communion of the Holy [Spirit], be with you all. Amen" (2 Cor. 13:14). This apostolic benediction places all members of the Trinity on an equal plane. The apostle's meaning is well summed up in 1 John 5:7, "For there are three that bear record in heaven, the Father, the Word, and the Holy [Spirit]: and these three are one."

Another way in which the Spirit's deity is known are by the attributes ascribed to Him:

Holiness (throughout Scripture He is called the *Holy* Spirit)—Ephesians 4:30
Truth—John 16:13
Life—Romans 8:2
Love—Romans 15:30
Eternity—Hebrews 9:14
Omnipotence (all-powerful)—Luke 1:35
Omniscience (all-knowing)—John 14:26; 16:13, 14; 1 Corinthians 2:10,11
Omnipresence (ever-present)—Psalm 139:7–10

The Holy Spirit is known to be deity from the performance of divine works:

He was involved in creation—Genesis 1:2; Psalm 104:30
He was involved in causing life—Genesis 2:7; Psalm 33:6; Job 27:3
He was the author of Scripture—2 Peter 1:21; 2 Timothy 3:16
He was the agent of Christ's incarnation—Luke 1:35
He was the agent of Christ's resurrection—Romans 8:11
He was the agent of regeneration—John 3:3, 5

A final area of proof for the deity of the Holy Spirit

are those Scripture passages where He is directly called God:

To lie to the Holy Spirit is to lie to God—Acts 5:3, 4
The Spirit of God—1 Corinthians 3:16
Your body is the Spirit's temple; glorify God!—1 Corinthians 6:19
Same Spirit, same Lord, same God—1 Corinthians 12:4-6
The Lord is that Spirit—the Spirit of the Lord—2 Corinthians 3:17, 18

Thus, the Holy Spirit is seen to be God by His identification with the Trinity, His possession of divine attributes and His performance of divine works. He is directly called God in Scripture.

III. The Holy Spirit's Special Ministry to Believers

The Church Age has been called the Age of the Spirit. The Holy Spirit has a unique relationship to the saints during the period from Pentecost until the Rapture. While this should make the doctrine of the Spirit of special interest to us of this age, the average Christian is ignorant of the Spirit's ministry.

We are first introduced to the Spirit's ministry when He, Who authored Scripture, uses it to bring us to conviction of sin and faith in Christ. Romans 10:17 declares, "Faith cometh by hearing, and hearing by the word of God." The Holy Spirit uses the Word to convict us of sin, righteousness and judgment (John 16:8). He leads us to acknowledge our sinfulness, repent and place our faith in Christ. He then uses the Scripture to bring assurance of our salvation by the grace of God. "Being confident of this very thing, that he which hath begun a good work in you will perform it until the day of Jesus Christ" (Phil. 1:6).

Having brought us to spiritual birth (John 3:5, 6), He now begins to teach us the truths of Scripture, which before were not discernible (1 Cor. 2:10-14). The author of Scripture becomes the chief teacher of Scripture for the believer.

"But the anointing which ye have received of him abideth in you, and ye need not that any man teach you: but as the same anointing teacheth you of all things, and is truth, and is no lie, and even as he hath taught you, ye shall abide in him" (1 John 2:27). Every believer is to test all teaching and preaching by the Scriptures and the inner ministry of the Holy Spirit (Acts 17:11).

To aid believers in knowing and understanding the Scriptures, the Holy Spirit gave several ministerial gifts to the church. These were the apostles, prophets, evangelists and pastor-teachers (Eph. 4:11, 12) who were to bring the saints to spiritual maturity so they could perform the work of the ministry and thereby build up the Body of Christ.

The Holy Spirit also gave sign gifts to the early church, which were a proof to the Jews primarily of the authenticity of the gospel message. When the gospel went to the Gentiles, who required no signs, and the canonization of written Scripture was complete, these gifts were discontinued. Ministry gifts such as service, teaching, exhortation, mercy, administration, faith, giving and prophecy were also given to aid the church-age believer in his service for Christ. It must be understood that the Holy Spirit is the ultimate source of all spiritual gifts. He does not give all gifts to any one Christian; nor may all gifts be found in every congregation. Our particular gifts will be best developed when we yield our lives to the daily control of the Holy Spirit, rather than anxiously trying to discern or develop them ourselves.

Since many today are confused about the Spirit's ministry, several terms need to be clarified:

1. The seal of the Spirit—Ephesians 1:13, 14; 4:30

The Greek term "seal" expressed ownership. Thus, the seal of the Spirit is God's claim of ownership and authority. It is also God's guarantee that our bodies will be resurrected on the day of redemption.

2. The baptism of the Spirit—1 Corinthians 12:13

Many have wrongly associated the baptism of the Spirit with "the second blessing," or speaking in tongues. All the verses in the Gospels and Acts focus on the day of Pentecost when the Holy Spirit began this dispensation. First Corinthians 12:13 is the only verse in the Bible that defines the baptism. Paul claims all believers are baptized into the Body of Christ. This event occurs once for each believer when he is born into God's family in salvation. It was not meant to be an emotional experience but an assurance that we are united as members of the Body of Christ.

3. The indwelling of the Spirit—1 Corinthians 3:16; 6:19

All born-again Christians since the day of Pentecost are permanently indwelt by the Holy Spirit. Absence of the Holy Spirit means a person is unsaved (Rom. 8:9). Since He permanently resides in our lives, sin will grieve Him until it is confessed (Eph. 4:30). The indwelling of the Holy Spirit brings the believer into fellowship with God.

4. The filling of the Spirit—Ephesians 5:18

While the indwelling of the Spirit is permanent, the filling of the Spirit results from the daily control of the Spirit in the Christian's life. Scripture commands the believer to be controlled by the Spirit. We will be filled by the Spirit when we surrender our bodies to God (Rom. 12:1, 2) as living sacrifices, and allow God to live through us (Gal. 2:20). Thus, we live daily in dependence upon God for a victorious, Spirit-controlled life.

5. The fruit of the Spirit—Galatians 5:22, 23

Rather than spiritual gifts, spiritual fruit is the true expression of a Spirit-filled life. When the life of the believer is surrendered to the control of the Spirit, the fruit of the Spirit becomes the expression of the indwelling Spirit.

Instead of looking for some unique experience, we

should be cultivating spiritual fruit. Jesus declared, "By their fruits ye shall know them" (Matt. 7:20). The fruit of the Spirit is the practical way to demonstrate the doctrine of the Spirit in our daily lives.

Research Bibliography

Bancroft, Emery H. *Christian Theology*. Grand Rapids: Zondervan, 1930.

Chafer, Lewis S. *Systematic Theology*. Vol. 1. Dallas: Dallas Seminary Press, 1978.

Evans, William. *The Great Doctrine of the Bible*. Chicago: Moody Press, 1974.

Gill, John. *Body of Divinity*. Book 1. Atlanta: Turner Lassetter, 1965.

Hodge, Charles. *Systematic Theology*. Vol. 1. New York: Charles Scribner's Sons, 1904.

Ryrie, Charles C. *A Survey of Bible Doctrine*. Chicago: Moody Press, 1972.

Strong, Augustus. *Systematic Theology*. Valley Forge, PA: Judson Press, 1960.

Questions for Research and Discussion

1. Research the Socinian concept of the Holy Spirit and contrast it with the Biblical doctrine to see how the Holy Spirit is a divine Person.
   - Where did these ideas originate?
   - What effect did this false doctrine have on the church?
   - How would you defend the Biblical doctrine?
2. Study the seven passages that refer to the baptism of the Holy Spirit (Matt. 3:11; Mark 1:8; Luke 3:16; John 1:33; Acts 11:16; 1 Cor. 12:13). Taking the one verse (1 Cor. 12:13) that defines the baptism of the Holy Spirit, determine:
   - How many Christians are baptized?
   - Baptized into what?
   - Why is the baptism of the Spirit misunderstood?

3. Why are some spiritual gifts no longer needed? Study 1 Corinthians 13:8–10.
4. What part does the Holy Spirit have in your prayer life? Study Romans 8:26, 27.
5. List several practical ways you can apply the doctrine of the Holy Spirit in your life.

Chapter 2

The Secrets and Evidences of a Spirit-Filled Life

Who needs the power of a Spirit-filled life? The young man whose inner life is passion-swept with temptation after temptation needs it. So does the young woman who is to keep free from the compromising enslavements of society. The businessman needs it to overcome the sly temptations of greed, selfishness and materialism. The store owner needs inner spiritual power to remove from the shelves and magazine racks those products of which he knows the Master disapproves. Both the student working for honors amid strong competition and the mechanic who desires to live an earnest, godly life in the shop need to be Spirit filled. The executive who would refrain from drinking and compromising to get ahead needs it. The preacher, when Spirit filled, will not be concerned about man's praise but God's approval. The mother needs this power to keep a sweet atmosphere within the home. The husband who desires to assume Biblical leadership in the home needs to be filled with the Holy Spirit. Let us not forget to add our names to this list of those needing the power of a Spirit-filled life.

I. The Power of a Spirit-Filled Life

We must remember that only born-again believers who surrender their lives to Christ can receive this power. It is important, therefore, to see the two things Christ came to earth to accomplish. He came, first, to save a powerless life and, second, to empower a saved life.

As the Lamb of God, Christ went to Calvary to shed His blood so our sins could be forgiven. The cross makes freedom from sin possible for those who place their faith in Christ for salvation. Christ is our Passover Lamb slain to cleanse us from all sin. He is our Savior and only hope for Heaven. Our faith in His finished work at Calvary brings us into the unique relationship of being members of God's family. We are assured of an eternity with God in Heaven.

But Christ came not only that we could go to Heaven when we died but also that we might have an abundant life here and now. He wants to empower every Christian through the Holy Spirit. The Spirit of God provides victory for the believer; He sets us free from the bondage and control of sin. As S. D. Gordon notes, "the Holy Spirit does *in* me what Christ did *for* me."[1]

The key to this spiritual power is the believer's surrender to the Holy Spirit. The Spirit must be able to work unhindered and unrestrained in our hearts. The result is that of which Paul spoke in Romans 15:13, "Now the God of hope fill you with all joy and peace in believing, that ye may abound in hope, through the power of the Holy [Spirit]."

II. The Secrets of a Spirit-Filled Life

Some years ago I was challenged to read the biographies of great Christians of the past and present. Having now read the life stories of almost a hundred great Spirit-filled men, I have noted three common secrets of their spiritual power and success:

1. Secret one: faith

Spirit-filled Christians have the common practice of walking by faith, not by sight (2 Cor. 5:7). Indeed, the Bible commands such a life of faith when it states, "The just shall live by faith" (Rom. 1:17). Not only are we saved by faith (Acts 16:31) and hold to solid doctrinal faith (Jude 3), but we are to live a life of faith.

Such a life reflects belief in God's Word. In Romans 4:20 and 22, Paul gives the example of Abraham who "staggered not at the promise of God through unbelief; but was strong in faith, giving glory to God; And being fully persuaded that, what he [God] had promised, he was able also to perform." The Scripture becomes the basis of thinking for the Spirit-filled individual. To walk by sight is to rely upon human logic, reasoning and resources, which most often have been defiled by the wrong programming of the world, the flesh and the devil. Christians are asked to have transformed thoughts and renewed minds. We need the new programming of the Scripture. This comes by believing and applying the principles, precepts and promises of the Word of God. Such a living faith moves us from the carnal life of the flesh, which is unacceptable to God (Rom. 8:4-8), to a walk or life in the Spirit.

This spiritual walk of faith is characterized by victory, spiritual maturity and inner peace. The victorious life is the norm for the Christian. It is the means of mental and emotional stability.

Faith gives the believer victory over sin. Paul tells us how to implement this faith in order to have victory over the flesh. "Likewise reckon ye also yourselves to be dead indeed unto sin, but alive unto God through Jesus Christ our Lord" (Rom. 6:11). We are to reckon (that is, by faith take it as a fact) that our old sinful nature is dead. When Christ died, our sin nature died. When Christ arose, our new nature was given life. By faith we understand these things to have happened in our lives the moment we became born-again Christians.

If the old nature is dead, why do we continue to sin after we are saved? The answer is our bodies and minds were programmed as a computer by the old nature, so when the stimulus of temptation comes, it is natural to yield. The only cure is to exercise spiritual control over the flesh. Therefore, we must yield ourselves to God and our members as instruments of righteousness (Rom. 6:13-23). When we sin, some member of the body is involved. It may be the hand, foot, eye or mouth. Faith brings these members of the body under the control of the Spirit of God. We can then claim with Paul, "For ye are dead, and your life is hid with Christ in God" (Col. 3:3). I remember Dick Harris once saying, "Faith is believing that God can do the impossible through me now." That is the first secret of a Spirit-filled life.

2. Secret two: a Christ-centered life

A second secret of those who enjoy the power of a Spirit-filled life is to know continuous personal fellowship with Christ. Note Christ's invitation in Matthew 11:28-30, "Come unto me . . . and I will give you rest . . . learn of me . . . and ye shall find rest unto your souls." Paul prayed that he would know Christ personally, "That I may know him, and the power of his resurrection . . ." (Phil. 3:10). He saw the great mystery of this age as "Christ in you, the hope of glory" (Col. 1:27). After the great chapter of faith, Hebrews 11, comes the apostolic admonition of Hebrews 12:1-3:

> Wherefore seeing we also are compassed about with so great a cloud of witnesses, let us lay aside every weight, and the sin which doth so easily beset us, and let us run with patience the race that is set before us, Looking unto Jesus the author and finisher of our faith; who for the joy that was set before him endured the cross, despising the shame, and is set down at the right hand of the throne of God. For consider him that endured such contradiction of sinners against himself, lest ye be wearied and faint in your minds.

We are to consider Him, or meditate upon His Person and work at Calvary. Hudson Taylor saw the importance of cherishing Christ through meditation as a spiritual key to holiness, joy, peace and victory.

There are some practical ways to make Christ the center of our lives. First, there is prayer. Jude tells us to be "praying in the [Spirit]." Ephesians 6:18 commands, "Praying always with all prayer and supplication in the Spirit. . . ." Through prayer our lives become interwoven with the Two Who intercede with the Father—Christ and the Spirit. Second, we become Christ-centered by studying the Scripture. Jesus taught that all Scripture points to Him (John 5:38, 39; 8:31, 32). The more we know the Bible, the more we can know Him. Thirdly, our trials can bring us to know Christ. James pictures our trials as the means of patience and spiritual growth and calls us to rejoice in them (James 1:2-4). Peter reminds us to cast all our care (anxiety) upon Him (1 Pet. 5:7). The more we practice these matters, the more personally we know Him; and the more personally we know Him, the more central He will be in our lives.

3. Secret three: surrender

The biographies of Spirit-filled Christians usually include a moment of total surrender to Christ apart from their salvation experience. This was not a second blessing nor an emotional high but a climax to a time of spiritual struggle. It was a once-and-for-all surrender to Christ as Lord and Master as described in Romans 12:1 and 2, "I beseech you therefore, brethren, by the mercies of God, that ye present [once for all] your bodies a living sacrifice, holy, acceptable unto God, which is your reasonable service. And be not conformed to this world: but be ye transformed by the renewing of your mind, that ye may prove what is that good, and acceptable, and perfect, will of God."

In these biographies, this total yielding of a life to the Holy Spirit was then followed by a daily desire to be Spirit filled. Ephesians 5:18 says to "be [continually] filled with the Spirit." This speaks of the control of the Holy Spirit in our lives. We must let Christ, through the power of the Spirit, live

His life through us. Paul sums it up this way, "I am crucified with Christ: nevertheless I live; yet not I, but Christ liveth in me: and the life which I now live in the flesh I live by the faith of the Son of God, who loved me, and gave himself for me" (Gal. 2:20).

Many years ago, in a revival meeting in Chattanooga, the speaker challenged us to surrender our lives to the power of a Spirit-filled life. He suggested we yield our lives to God by praying, "Father, show me anything in my life that is displeasing to you. Show me anything you would change. By your grace helping me, I will put it out, whatever the cost. I now appropriate by faith the power of the Holy Spirit in me to glorify Jesus Christ." Many went through the spiritual struggle which led to total surrender to Christ and the Spirit-filled life.

III. The Evidences of a Spirit-Filled Life

Since our spiritual surrender makes Christ Lord of our lives, one evidence of the Spirit-filled life is Christ's glorification. Jesus presented the major ministry of the Spirit as glorifying Him. One reason we know that much of the modern idea of the Holy Spirit's work is Scripturally wrong is the emphasis on the Spirit Himself. The Holy Spirit never seeks to glorify Himself but Christ alone: "he shall testify of me" (John 15:26); "he shall not speak of himself" (John 16:13); "He shall glorify me" (John 16:14). Since the Holy Spirit focuses all attention on Christ, when the Spirit is in control of our lives we will glorify Christ as Lord. Paul taught that no one could call Jesus "Lord" apart from the Holy Spirit within him (1 Cor. 12:3). When He is Lord of our lives we will seek to show it by obedience to His will and His Word.

A second evidence of a Spirit-filled life is love for fellow believers. There are good reasons for us to love other Christians:

We all serve the same Master—Matthew 23:8

We all have the same Father—John 1:12, 13
Love for fellow Christians is a mark of true spiritual birth—John 4:12; 5:1
We are all heirs of the same inheritance—Romans 8:16, 17
We have been bought with the same price, the blood of Christ—1 Corinthians 6:20
We have been baptized into the same body, the Body of Christ—1 Corinthians 12:13
We are all walking the same pathway of faith—2 Corinthians 5:7

Jesus put it this way, "By this shall all men know that ye are my disciples, if ye have love one to another" (John 13:35).

Too many churches allow carnal believers to disrupt the unity of the body by bitterness, gossip and evil reports. True revival results when carnality is disciplined and the majority of believers in the church are Spirit filled.

A third evidence of a Spirit-filled life is soul-winning power. When Jesus promised the coming of the Holy Spirit to the disciples it was connected to witnessing. "Ye shall receive power, after that the Holy [Spirit] is come upon you: and ye shall be witnesses unto me . . ." (Acts 1:8). Solomon said, "The fruit of the righteous is a tree of life; and he that winneth souls is wise" (Prov. 11:30). The psalmist declares, "They that sow in tears shall reap in joy. He that goeth forth and weepeth, bearing precious seed, shall doubtless come again with rejoicing, bringing his sheaves with him" (Ps. 126: 5, 6). Those whose lives are characterized as Spirit-filled are also noted for their soul-winning burden, compassion and efforts, sure marks of the Spirit's control of one's life.

Finally, we must examine the major evidence of the Spirit-filled life. Jesus has said, "By their fruits ye shall know them" (Matt. 7:20). What fruit? Certainly the fruit of soul winning and abiding in Christ is included. But how is that fruit of abiding in Christ described? Paul lists the nine aspects of the fruit of the Spirit in Galatians 5:22 and 23. We shall study them more in the next chapter, and the chapters that follow will deal with each aspect individually. For now we shall simply list them and make a brief comment about each one.

1. Love - God yearning over a lost and broken world through us—2 Corinthians 5:14, 15
2. Joy - evidence of the abundant life provided by the grace of God—John 10:10; Luke 15:7, 10
3. Peace - the peace of God actively overcoming all anxiety and difficult circumstances—Philippians 4:6, 7
4. Longsuffering - God's demonstration of His infinite patience with those who are in opposition to His will—2 Peter 3:9, 15
5. Gentleness - God's loving-kindness shown through us to those who are unlovely and unworthy—Titus 3:2-6
6. Goodness - God's love actively expressed through us by unselfishness—1 Corinthians 10:30-33; Romans 2:4
7. Faith - evidence to the world of the trustworthiness of God's promises—Acts 11:23, 24
8. Meekness - demonstration of our submission to God's discipline—2 Corinthians 10:1, 3-5
9. Temperance (self-control) - evidence that we are controlled by the Spirit and not by self—1 Corinthians 9:24-27

Research Bibliography

Chambers, J. Oswald. *Conformed to His Image*. Ft. Washington, PA: Christian Literature Crusade, 1963.

Edman, V. Raymond. *They Found the Secret*. Grand Rapids: Zondervan, 1970.

Erdman, W. J. *The Holy Spirit and Christian Experience*. New York: Gospel Publishing House, 1909.

Gardner, George. *The Corinthian Catastrophe*. Grand Rapids: Kregel Publications, 1974.

Gromacki, Robert G. *The Modern Tongues Movement*. Phillipsburg, NJ: Presbyterian and Reformed Publishing, (Baker Book House, Distributor), 1972.

Legters, L. L. *God's Provision for Victorious Living*. Philadelphia: Christian Life Literature Fund, 1935.

Ryrie, Charles C. *The Holy Spirit*. Chicago: Moody Press, 1970.

Questions for Research and Discussion

1. Do a study of Romans 6:11-22. Note the difference between "yield yourselves" and "yield ye your members." Relate "yield yourselves" to the once-for-all presentation or surrender of Romans 12:1. Relate "yield ye your members" to the daily surrender to the control of the Holy Spirit as in Ephesians 5:18.
2. Discuss the Lordship of Christ in the life of the believer. How can you make Christ Lord of your life?
3. What is the life of faith and how does it relate to walking in the Spirit?
4. What is a Spirit-filled life and why is the fruit of the Spirit better evidence of it than the so-called spiritual gifts?
5. What are the other evidences of a Spirit-filled life? Do you show these in your life? If not, how do you plan to cultivate them?

Chapter 3

Understanding the Fruit of the Spirit

The area of our third pastorate abounded with apple, pear, cherry and peach orchards. We would often drive past miles of these carefully cultivated trees, row after row arranged in exact order. Fruit from these trees did not grow and ripen overnight but as a result of sunshine and rain, watchful care and pruning. Those who were responsible for the development of the fruit combined study with hard work, training with constant care. Only then would the results of their efforts be rewarded. So it is with spiritual fruit.

Since the fruit of the Spirit is the primary evidence of a Spirit-controlled life, we need to study to understand the nature of the fruit. We need to train to be able to cultivate it in our lives. It will take hard work, constant care and effort, but the results will be eternally rewarding.

I. The Fruit Contrasted with the Lust of the Flesh

When Paul presents the nine aspects of the fruit of the Spirit, he contrasts them with the works and lust of the flesh (Gal. 5:16-26). He shows that the Christian who walks in the Spirit will not fulfill the lust of the flesh but will cultivate the fruit of the Spirit (v. 16). He then describes the conflict between the flesh and the Holy Spirit in the believer's life (v. 17). It is impossible to combine the two life-styles of spirituality and carnality. To attempt to do so results in hypocrisy, one of the main problems of Christians today. Jesus spoke of this as a problem of the Laodicean age, "I know thy works, that thou art neither cold nor hot: I would thou wert cold or hot. So then because thou art lukewarm, and neither cold nor hot, I will spue thee out of my mouth" (Rev. 3:15, 16). No one is as sick of hypocrites as God.

The carnal life-style of the flesh is described (Gal. 5:19-21) in such terms as:

Adultery - unfaithfulness in marriage
Fornication - any sensual or sexual indulgence
Uncleanness - sinful lusts and sodomy
Lasciviousness - indecent, unrestrained and shameless conduct
Idolatry - the worship of idols, images and materialism
Witchcraft - involvement in occult practices
Hatred - holding bitterness and anger toward others
Variance - causing division and discord
Emulations - a burning jealousy
Wrath - uncontrolled anger, a hot temper
Strife - debating contentiously with enmity
Seditions - causing dissension by false teaching
Heresies - a self-willed opinion contrary to Scripture
Envyings - feeling displeasure over others' advantages
Murders - taking another's life by deed or thought
Drunkenness - being under the control of intoxicants or drugs
Revelings - uncontrolled rioting and pleasure making
And such like - the list continues indefinitely

Similar lists should be studied for comparison and additions. Some passages are: Matthew 15:17-20; Romans 1:21-32; 1 Corinthians 6:9-11; Ephesians 4:29-31; Colossians 3:1-10; 2 Timothy 3:1-8; Revelation 21:8. For our present study, consider how the fruit of the Spirit contrasts with the lust of the flesh in the following chart.

	Fruit of the Spirit ← compared with →	Lust of the flesh
IN-WARD	Love	Hatred
	Joy	Revelings
	Peace	Strife, variance, emulations
OUT-WARD	Longsuffering	Wrath
	Gentleness	Murders (meanness)
	Goodness	Adultery, fornication, uncleanness, lasciviousness
GOD-WARD	Faith	Idolatry, witchcraft, seditions, heresies
	Meekness	Envyings
	Self-Control	Drunkenness

It is important for every Christian to become familiar with these contrasts and to spend time meditating on the use of Scriptural fruit to overcome the fleshly lust. You will have noticed in the preceding chart a three-fold division of the fruit of the Spirit—inward fruit bearing, outward fruit bearing and God-ward fruit bearing. Let us examine them.

II. The Three Directions of Fruit Bearing

Perhaps you noticed that the *works* of the flesh is plural while the *fruit* of the Spirit is singular. The explanation for this is found in the unified nature of spiritual fruit. There are not nine different fruits of the Spirit; there is one fruit expressed by nine aspects. We either have all nine aspects evident in our lives or we have none. Spiritual fruit is a result of a Spirit-filled life. When we are controlled by the Holy Spirit, He will display His fruit in our lives. We are fruit bearing because He is living Christ's life through us. It is well, then, to note three directions to this fruit bearing.

1. Inward fruit bearing

The first three aspects of the fruit of the Spirit are those that affect our mental and emotional health. Love helps us to overcome selfishness. It focuses on God, spiritual things and other people, keeping us from being self-centered. Joy deals with our self-pity, providing inner satisfaction. True joy does not depend upon people, circumstances or things. Peace gives mental and emotional contentment and control to our lives so that we overcome depression, despondency and despair. Perhaps the following chart will help clarify the inward direction of fruit bearing.

Love
instead of
selfishness
1 John 4:10-13

(The *E* stands for Ego.)

Joy
instead of
self-pity
Romans 14:17-19

Peace
instead of
despair
Philippians 4:6, 7

2. Outward fruit bearing

The middle three aspects of the fruit of the Spirit affect our actions. While we know emotionally whether we have love, joy and peace, others will know by our actions and attitudes whether we have longsuffering, gentleness and goodness. Longsuffering, which means to be long-tempered, will keep us from becoming impatient and angry. Gentleness translates our inner peace into kind actions. It erases irritability in our relations with others. Goodness produces a mature life-style free from malice. It puts the holiness of Christ into action within our lives. This next chart is given to help you better understand the outward direction of fruit bearing.

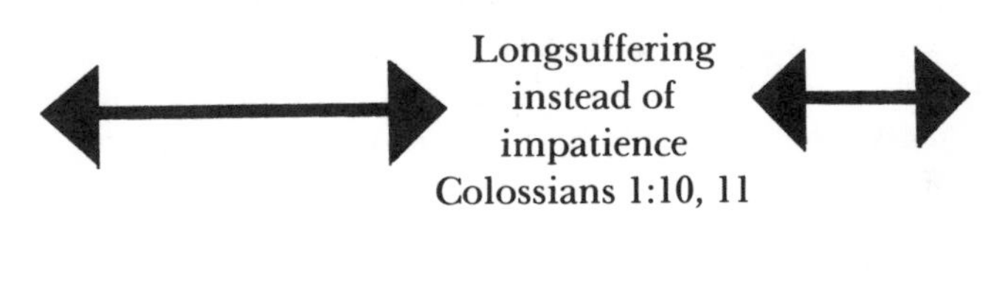

Longsuffering
instead of
impatience
Colossians 1:10, 11

Gentleness
instead of
irritability
2 Timothy 2:23, 24

Goodness
instead of
malice
Romans 15:13, 14

3. God-ward fruit bearing

The last three aspects of spiritual fruit relate primarily to God. Other people, and even we ourselves, may not be totally aware that we exercise them. We are the best judges of love, joy and peace. Others will certainly judge us on longsuffering, gentleness and goodness. But God is the judge of faithfulness, meekness and self-control. Faith, or faithfulness, keeps our lives true to the Word of God as God reveals it to us. We are not only to hear the Word but to practice it faithfully. Meekness is true humility. It keeps us from an ungodly dogmatism. Only God knows if we are humble. Self-control or temperance brings stability to our lives and keeps us from irrational compulsiveness. God will judge whether this aspect of spiritual fruit will merit a reward in Heaven (1 Cor. 9:25). These three aspects of the fruit of the Spirit are used by God to affect our temperaments. The following chart is given to help you develop a better comprehension of the God-ward direction of fruit bearing.

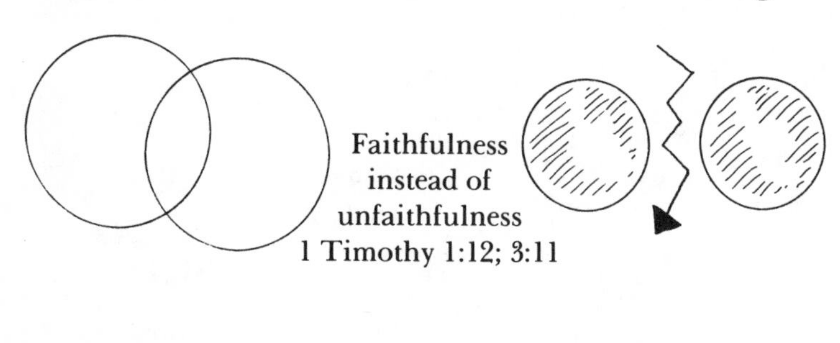

III. Understanding Spiritual Fruit

It is the desire of Christ that His true disciples be fruit-bearers. In John 15:8 He declares, "Herein is my Father glorified, that ye bear much fruit; so shall ye be my disciples." God did not save us so we could live carnal life-styles. He planned from eternity that we should display the fruit of a Spirit-controlled life. John 15:16 says, "Ye have not chosen me, but I have chosen you, and ordained you, that ye should go and bring forth fruit, and that your fruit should remain. . . ." Such fruit bearing is a result of abiding in Christ.

Successful fruit bearing demands that a proper fellowship with God be carefully maintained. This means that we must avoid anything that would break our fellowship with the Holy Spirit. Since He permanently indwells the Christian, He will not leave. But sinful attitudes can grieve Him (Eph. 4:30), and sinful actions can quench or turn off His power (1 Thess. 5:19-23).

To be effective fruit-bearers we must seek to be Christlike. This means putting to death the lusts and works of the flesh (Gal. 5:24), living and walking in constant fellowship with the Holy Spirit (Gal. 5:25) and allowing Him to sow His seed in our lives (Gal. 6:8), which we then have the task of cultivating to full maturity.

When I lived along the East Coast, I noticed that several houses from Boston to Virginia had the distinction "George Washington slept here." Perhaps when we have fully cultivated the fruit of the Spirit in our lives, we will gain the much more important distinction "the Holy Spirit lives here."

Research Bibliography

Chadwick, Samuel. *The Way to Pentecost.* Berne, IN: Light and Hope Publications, 1937.

LaHaye, Tim. *Spirit-Controlled Temperament.* Wheaton, IL: Tyndale House, 1976.

MacArthur, John Jr. *Living in the Spirit.* Panorama City, CA: Word of Grace Communications, 1981.

Orr, J. Edwin. *Full Surrender.* Edinburg: Marshall, Morgan and Scott, 1967.

Rees, Tom. *The Spirit of Life.* Chicago: Moody Press, n.d.

Strauss, Lehman. *Be Filled with the Spirit.* Grand Rapids: Zondervan, 1976.

Questions for Research and Discussion

1. Why is the "fruit of the Spirit" singular and not plural (i.e., "fruits")? Relate this to our being filled with the Spirit. Relate it also to our reaction to people, circumstances and things.
2. Do you understand how the various aspects of the fruit of the Spirit are organized and relate to each other? Review and discuss this subject, particularly as it contrasts with the lust of the flesh.
3. Discuss the conditions for spiritual fruit bearing and how we can meet them in practical ways in our daily lives.
4. Make a list of things in your life that grieve or quench the Holy Spirit. What aspect of spiritual fruit would you use most to effect change in each area?

5. Keep a record of actual sins you commit this week. Note what aspect of spiritual fruit was violated when you sinned. Notice how sin affects our spiritual lives and how attention to the fruit of the Spirit can bring us to greater spiritual victory.

Chapter 4

The Fruit of the Spirit is

LOVE

A young teenage girl was noted for her grace and purity of character. She wore a little gold locket almost all of the time and would never let anyone see what was inside. One day a friend simply touched it and it fell open. Inside were written the words, "Whom having not seen, I love," referring to the Lord Jesus Christ. That was the secret of her spiritual character, which made her different from many other people. "Whom having not seen, I love."

Many times we are told that we need to have the fruit of the Spirit in our lives: love, joy, peace, longsuffering, gentleness, goodness, faith, meekness and temperance. We should not be surprised to find that the very first aspect of the fruit of the Spirit is love. The word "love" is often misunderstood and misapplied today. What does it really mean? What is the fruit of the Spirit which is love? How do we display that particular aspect of spiritual fruit within our lives?

I. The Basis of Spiritual Character

To understand the spiritual character of love, we need to study 1 Corinthians 13:8-13, where we see fourteen characteristics of God's love.

There are several Greek words that are translated by the one English word "love." *Phileo* is friendship love.

Some years ago, I lived in Philadelphia, the city of brotherly love. Brotherly love is a good definition of this Greek word *phileo.* But *phileo* is not the word that we have in 1 Corinthians 13. The word *eros* refers to the love of a husband and wife. But that is not the word Paul uses for love. Rather, he uses the word *agape* which is God's type of love, divine love.

When God asks us to have the fruit of the Spirit in our lives, He is not asking us to have friendship love or marital love but God's divine love. That is the measuring rod.

Many people are so full of the twentieth century terminology that they never fully comprehend what God's love is all about. If a person has God's love active in his life, he will have better friendships and a better marriage. He will be able to solve work problems much more easily. He needs God's love as the basis of his character. Notice these fourteen spiritual characteristics of the love of God. Use this list each day to see where you fail to display the fruit of the Spirit which is love.

1. Love is longsuffering

"Love suffers long." God's love is longsuffering; it does not give up easily. It just keeps going and going and going. It acts with patience and understanding.

2. Love is kind

Are you a kind person? If I were to go into a home and ask a four-year-old child if his mommy and daddy loved each other, he would probably always say yes, because mommy and daddy are supposed to love each other. But if I asked, "Are your mommy and daddy friends?" I would find out the honest situation of the home. Sometimes the child would answer, "Oh yes, they are." Other times he would say, "Not yesterday!" Love is kind. Love is courteous.

3. Love is not envious

Envy is looking at someone else and wishing we could be like them. Have you ever thought as you looked in the mirror in the morning, "If only I could look like so and so, then I would have friends"? But we have friends not because we look a certain way but because of our inward character. Envy cuts off and destroys friendship, but the fruit of love builds it.

4. Love is not proud

The number one sin that the Bible presents for every individual is the sin of pride. In the book of Hebrews it is "the sin which doth so easily beset us." Pride promotes almost all the other sins. Adam and Eve were lifted up in pride before they were disobedient. We need to replace pride with God's love, which is not proud.

5. Love behaves itself properly

Love promotes proper behavior. Love knows how to live with ethics and morality. Christ has a refining influence upon the believer, changing him into a new creation by the power of the Holy Spirit. The person who knows Christ best will display proper actions and behavior.

6. Love is not selfish

"Love seeks not her own." Love does not have selfish gain and advantages in mind. When love controls the heart, the individual will put others first, self-will last. Love provides for others and looks out for their interests.

7. Love is not provoked

Have you ever been provoked? "Be angry and sin not," is a command of Scripture. This means, literally, that we must be angry only with sin. We must not be angry, or provoked, at an individual, even if we are mistreated. We may become angry at the sin that is done but never at the person doing the sinning. An unChrist-like anger is always sin. When a Christian becomes angry with his brother in Christ, he sins. Note some things anger will cause. Anger causes friction, or problems, between individuals. Anger can also cause a faction, or division, among a group of people. Anger is a picture of an unstable life, a life that is not able to cope with situations. It is a sign that a person is not truly yielded to the Lord Jesus Christ and the work of the Holy Spirit within his life.

8. Love does not think evil

"Love thinketh no evil." Have you ever had evil thoughts of another person, enough to wish evil on him? Sometimes when God chastens a person, others gloat and say, "I knew that was going to happen." We need to be very careful. Love credits others with the best possible motives rather than offering sharp critical judgments.

9. Love rejoices in the truth, not in sin

"Love rejoiceth not in iniquity, but rejoiceth in the truth." Love does not rejoice when evil happens to another. It rejoices in righteousness. God's love is centered in the truth of the written Word and the living Word.

10. Love bears all things

Love is a burden bearer. The person who cultivates God's love will seek to lift up the lives of others, not tear them down. He will constructively build them up and edify them in the truth of the Word of God.

11. Love believes the best of other people

"Love believeth all things." When someone brings you a rumor, do you believe it? Many people do. "Oh, so and so told me." Rumors spread fast. Wisdom reminds us to believe nothing of what we hear and only half of what we see—a good rule to follow regarding rumors and evil reports. Love believes the best of the other person.

12. Love hopes the best for other people

Love rejoices in another's promotions and advancements. When God lifts someone else up, it is better to praise the Lord for what He is doing in that person's life than to let envy come in and destroy.

13. Love endures all things

"Love endureth all things." Love puts up with many things. Love would rather patiently endure than become bitter and hateful. How enduring are you?

14. Love does not give up

"Love never faileth." Literally it means that love does not give up. It does not abandon ship. It just keeps going on. Love is permanent and concrete.

The Buddhists have a saying, "If you will think of Buddha you will soon be like Buddha." Christians find that Scripture teaches something similar but superior. If we meditate on the Lord Jesus Christ and His character of love, we will soon be cultivating all these fourteen characteristics of love in our lives. The basis of all spiritual character is this fruit of the Spirit which is love.

II. The Basis of Spiritual Testimony

Love is the basis of spiritual testimony. In John 13:34 and 35, Jesus said, "A new commandment I give unto you, That ye love one another; as I have loved you, that ye also love one another. By this shall all men know that ye are my disciples, if ye have love one to another." The Christian who cultivates the fruit of love will have a testimony of forgiveness. He will love other people the way Jesus loves him.

Have you ever thought of what it means for Christ to love us? He loves sinners, wicked and depraved. Sin is repulsive and ugly to a holy God, but because He loves us He wants to change our lives.

When we come across an ugly character whose disposition is not gentle, we are repelled. We should be praying, "Lord, help me to minister to that person and to be a solution to his problems." If someone is irritable, he has a spiritual problem to which we must minister with the love of God.

We are to forgive others as He forgave us. Both Ephesians and Colossians have statements regarding this forgiving love that becomes the basis of our spiritual testimony. Ephesians 4:32 says, "And be ye kind one to another, tenderhearted, forgiving one another, even as God for Christ's sake hath forgiven you." That is a tall order. Remember, we were wicked, vile, helpless, depraved sinners when God set His love upon us. His grace drew us to Calvary, where we repented of our sin and exercised faith in the Lord Jesus Christ, thereby being born again into His family. God, for Christ's sake, forgave us and took our sin away as far as the east is from the west. Now He wants us to act the same way in relation to others.

One lady told me she had forgiven a particular person but could never forget what he had done. She could not fulfill God's desire to erase that person's deed from her mind. Peter asked, "Lord, should I forgive my brother seven times?" He answered, "Seventy times seven," or four hundred and ninety times. Have you ever forgiven anyone that many times? If we could forgive someone four hundred and ninety times it would change our lives. God's basis for forgiving a person is to let him know that you love him and forgive him. We are to minister the fruit of love to people in order to change their lives and develop their spiritual character.

Colossians 3:12–14 commands, "Put on therefore, as the elect of God, holy and beloved, bowels of mercies, kindness, humbleness of mind, meekness, longsuffering; Forbearing one another, and forgiving one another, if any man have a quarrel against any: even as Christ forgave you, so also do ye. And above all these things put on charity, which is the bond of perfectness." Notice how many of the characteristics of God's love from 1 Corinthians 13 are mentioned in these two passages on forgiveness. To find them is not as difficult as to apply them.

The word "quarrel" is the Greek word for embitterment. When something makes us a little bitter toward another person, we are to forgive him as Christ forgave us. Don Loney once said that the church is the only institution on earth that kills its wounded. Sometimes that is too true. We ought to take a wounded soul, put on the balm of Gilead and restore him to spiritual health. The church should be the most forgiving institution in the world because the love of God is shed abroad in our hearts by the Holy Spirit.

Not only should we have a testimony of forgiveness by having this fruit of love in our lives but also a testimony of discipleship. John 13:35 says, "By this shall all men know that ye are my disciples, if ye have love one to another." All men, saved and unsaved, will know that we belong to Christ, because we show the characteristic of divine love. Someone has written:

> You are writing a gospel, a chapter each day,
> By deeds that you do, by words that you say.
> Men read what you write, whether faithless or true.
> Say, what is the gospel according to you?
> Men read and admire the gospel of Christ,
> With its love so unfailing and true;
> But what do they say, and what do they think
> Of the gospel according to you?

Do others look at us and say, "That person is a disciple of Jesus Christ, molding his life to be like Jesus and exhibiting to me the forgiveness of God"?

III. The Basis of Spiritual Fruit

Love Begins the Progression

Love → Joy → Peace → Longsuffering → Gentleness → Goodness ↴

Self-Control ← Meekness ← Faith

The fruit of love is the basis of all other aspects of spiritual fruit. Love begins the progression of the fruit of the Spirit. "The fruit of the Spirit is love, joy, peace, longsuffering, gentleness, goodness, faith, meekness, temperance, against such there is no law." If I have God's love in my life, it will produce joy. If I have God's love and joy in my life, they will produce peace. If I have love, joy and peace in my life, they will produce longsuffering, gentleness and goodness. These will then produce faith, meekness and temperance. You see, all of the aspects of spiritual fruit depend on the beginning point of love. If we do not begin with love, we will never have peace, joy, humility or self-control (temperance). A lack of self-control is a true sign of a lack of God's love.

Love is a Three-way Street

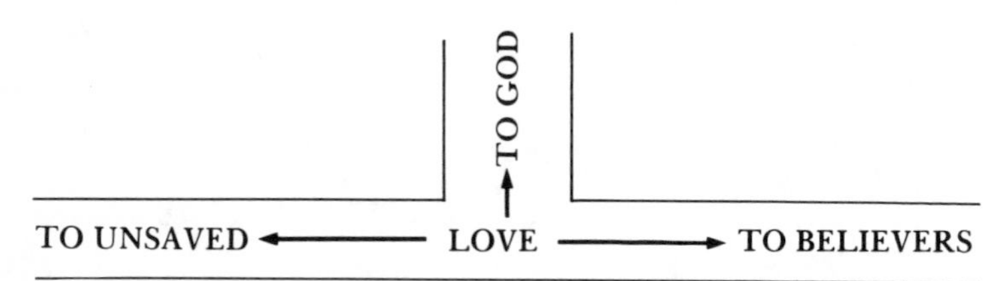

Love is a three-way street. We are to display love to God, to fellow believers and to the unsaved. Our love to God is seen in 1 John 4:19, "We love him, because he first loved us." Isn't it wonderful that God loved us! We would not have loved Him unless He first loved us. We need to direct our love to God by telling Him that we love Him. I was thrilled to hear someone in his prayer telling God how much he loved Him. Love cannot remain silent. When did you last tell the Lord that you loved Him?

After God says "we love him because he first loved us," He states in 1 John 4:20 and 21, "If a man say, I love God, and hateth his brother, he is a liar: for he that loveth not his brother whom he hath seen, how can he love God whom he hath not seen? And this commandment have we from him, That he who loveth God love his brother also."

We must not only say "Lord, I love You," but we must show God that we love Him by loving other believers and bearing their burdens. We will then be fulfilling the characteristics of God's love from 1 Corinthians 13.

Then we are to love the unsaved. "The love of Christ constraineth us," Paul said in 2 Corinthians 5:14. He was burdened for people to come to Christ because of the love of God in his heart. Do we have that love that reaches out to lost, eternal, living souls with a burden that they come to Christ? Until our hearts have that burden we will not have fully cultivated the fruit of the Spirit which is love.

Research Bibliography

Drummond, Henry. *The Greatest Thing in the World.* London: Collins, 1960.

Gage, Robert. *The Birthmarks of the Christian Life* (chap. 4). Grand Rapids: Sword & Shield Ministries, 1976.

Getz, Gene A. *Building Up One Another.* Wheaton, IL: Victor Books, 1976.

Lewis, C. S. *Our Four Loves.* New York: Harcourt Brace, Inc., 1960.

Richards, Larry. *Becoming One in the Spirit.* New York: Pyramid Publications, 1973.

Sweeting, George. *Love is the Greatest.* Chicago: Moody Press, 1974.

Questions for Research and Discussion

1. Use this self-check list on the characteristics of God's love to discover areas needing improvement. Develop a plan for improving each weak area.

Characteristic of love	**How can I improve?**
☐ Longsuffering	
☐ Kindness	
☐ Not envious	
☐ Not proud	
☐ Behaves properly	
☐ Not self-willed	
☐ Not provoked	
☐ Does not think evil of others	
☐ Rejoices in truth, not in sins of others	
☐ Bears others' burdens	
☐ Believes best for others	
☐ Hopes best for others	
☐ Endures all things	
☐ Never gives up	

2. Discuss how love is the basis for all other aspects of spiritual fruit.
3. Discuss how love works in three directions: toward God, toward fellow believers and toward the unsaved. Make a list of three things you can do to cultivate love in each of these directions.

Toward God	**Toward believers**	**Toward unsaved**
1.	1.	1.
2.	2.	2.
3.	3.	3.

4. Why is it so important for Christians to show their love to fellow believers? Search John 13:34, 35; Ephesians 4:32; Colossians 3:12–14 for the answers.
5. Make a list of practical ways you can show the fruit of love in your basic interpersonal relationships.
   Your mate

Your family—parents, brothers, sisters
Your children or grandchildren
Your best friend
Your schoolmates or fellow workers
Your neighbors
A person you dislike or usually seek to avoid

Chapter 5

The Fruit of the Spirit is

JOY

There once was a Christian cobbler in Germany who often sat working outside the door of his little cobbler shop. He would often sing with joy and gratitude his thanksgiving to God. One day a Jewish man walking by heard the cobbler singing and asked, "Why are you so happy?" The cobbler said, "The reason I have joy is that I am the King's son." He made no explanation and the Jewish man went away thinking, "This fellow is crazy. If he were the King's son, he wouldn't be working in a cobbler's shop but living in prosperity." The cobbler realized he probably should have made an explanation. When the man came by again, he said, "I explained that my joy was because I was the King's son, but I did not explain to you who the King was." He presented the Lord Jesus Christ and what the Word of God says regarding salvation. That Jewish man was lead by the humble cobbler to faith in the Lord Jesus Christ, and he went away with the fruit of the Spirit which is joy.

One of the distinguishing features of a New Testament church is its singing. The Bible says we are to make a joyful noise unto the Lord. Not only can the sopranos, altos, tenors, baritones and basses sing, but also those who have just one note can make a joyful noise unto the Lord.

Some years ago on Word of Life Island, if Robbie Robertson saw somebody who did not look too happy, he would ask, "Have you lost the joy?" The way he would look at the person would put a big smile on the person's face. Robbie would then say, "Oh, you got it back." He was so thrilled with his own Christian life experience he wanted everyone to have the joy. Suppose someone came to you and asked, "Have you lost the joy?" What would you say?

Each aspect of the fruit of the Spirit is dependent upon the previous one. You cannot have joy without love. When the love of God is spread abroad in hearts by the Holy Spirit, the joy of the Christian life will be evident. We will have joy even in the darkest circumstances and most difficult trials. Since most modern Americans are not looking for joy, but happiness, we need to distinguish between the two. Wendell Loveless said, "It is not mere happiness that God gives, it is joy. Happiness depends on happenings. But joy transcends circumstances and finds its source in Christ."[1]

People look for happiness everywhere. For some it is in materialism. Others spend hours daily watching television. Still others seek the thrills of an amusement park. But the human resources for happiness fail to provide true joy. They leave us just as empty as when we started. People aim at happiness and miss real joy because Christ is the only true source of joy. Look at what some great people of the Bible said:

David—Rejoice in the Lord, O ye righteous.
Isaiah—Thou shalt rejoice in the Lord.
Joel—Be glad and rejoice in the Lord your God.
Paul—Rejoice and again I say rejoice.
Peter—Rejoice with joy unspeakable and full of glory.

Joy is the result of having experienced God's love in our lives and realizing that it lifts us up past worldly pleasures and happiness into a higher realm. Have you lost the joy? Perhaps we should ask, Have you ever found the joy?

I. The Joy of Salvation from Sin

Joy begins with salvation from sin.

Christ, in the parable of Matthew 13, gives a hint of where joy begins. He speaks of the person who hears the Word and receives it with joy. I can remember when I did not know the way of salvation. I thought it difficult to read the Bible with all its genealogies, long names and seeming archaic expressions. I said, "How can anyone ever understand the Bible?" Then God showed me that I was a lost sinner headed toward hell with no hope of Heaven. As I recognized my depravity, He told me that He had already done something about my sin problem by sending the Lord Jesus Christ to die in my place. He revealed through the Bible that I had to call upon the name of the Lord to be saved. As I renounced my sins and put my faith in the Son of God, that was joy. I experienced the true joy of the gospel. But that was just the beginning.

Isaiah 12:3 says, "Therefore with joy shall ye draw water out of the wells of salvation." When the woman of Samaria came face to face with the Lord Jesus Christ, He offered her the water of life freely. After she accepted Christ as the Son of God, she ran into the city and told people about this Man she had met at the well of Jacob, Who gave her the water of life. She introduced the whole city to Christ because she was filled with the joy of what had happened in her own life. Paul declares, "Now the God of hope fill you with all joy and peace in believing, that ye may abound in hope, through the power of the Holy [Spirit]" (Rom. 15:13).

When God reveals His Word to us, there is joy. When we draw water from the well of salvation, there is joy. After we have believed the gospel, the joy of the Holy Spirit is within our lives. The joy of salvation is expressed by Isaiah, "The ransomed of the LORD shall return, and come to Zion with songs and everlasting joy upon their heads: they shall obtain joy and gladness, and sorrow and sighing shall flee away" (Isa. 35:10). This is the joy of being saved.

Did you know there is joy in Heaven when someone is saved? In Luke 15:7 and 10 Jesus said, "I say unto you, that likewise joy shall be in heaven over one sinner that repenteth, more than over ninety and nine just persons, which need no repentance. Likewise, I say unto you, there is joy in the presence of the angels of God over one sinner that repenteth." Every time someone receives Christ as Savior there is singing up in Heaven. On the day you repented of your sin and put your faith in the Lord Jesus Christ, there was joy in Heaven over your salvation.

There is also joy every time a backslider gets right with God. Remember David's experience when he was confronted with his sin, failure and backsliding? God dealt with his heart by sending a prophet to convict him of his sin. When David recognized his awful sin he cried out, "Restore unto me the joy of thy salvation;. . ." (Ps. 51:12). He knew something was missing in his life. Everyone who walks away from fellowship with the Son of God loses his joy. Like David, he needs to cry to God, "Restore unto me the joy of thy salvation."

II. The Joy of Fellowship with God

Joy is developed in our Christian experience through fellowship with God. The greater our fellowship with God, the more we will cultivate joy. Psalm 16:11 says, "In thy presence is fulness of joy." Since God's presence is a place of joy, only as we walk in the presence of God, fellowshiping with Him, can we have His joy. If there is an absence of joy, we need to check on our fellowship with God.

John writes in his first epistle about fellowship. "That which was from the beginning, which we have heard, which we have seen with our eyes, which we have looked upon, and our hands have handled, of the Word of life" (1 John 1:1). John tells of that wonderful, personal fellowship he had had with the Son of God as His disciple. For three years, John had the privilege of going everywhere with Christ. He saw miracles performed such as the dead raised and blind people receiving their sight. He saw God's holiness in an outward display and knew what it was to be in the presence of the Holy One of Israel. Now he says, "For the life was manifested, and we have seen it, and bear witness, and show unto you that eternal life, which was with the Father, and was manifested unto us; That which we have seen and heard declare we unto you, that ye also may have fellowship with us: and truly our fellowship is with the Father, and with his Son Jesus Christ" (1 John 1:2, 3). We can experience the same fellowship John experienced with Christ. Notice the result of this fellowship, "These things write we unto you, that your joy may be full." Fellowship in the presence of God brings fullness of joy.

Joy also comes through our abiding in Christ. In John 15:11, after Christ has spoken of abiding in Him, we read, "These things have I spoken unto you, that my joy might remain in you, and that your joy might be full." The key to full joy is abiding in Christ. Do we have our roots down deep in the very Person of Christ? Is He our source of strength and encouragement? Many Christians remain defeated and discouraged because they look to man for encouragement. When they have problems to solve they depend on fellowship with the individual who is counseling them. While we need the encouragement of others, we need to see the very Person of Christ as our chief source of encouragement so we can be triumphant. He will be with us in the lonely hours because He never leaves us nor forsakes us. We need to be abiding in Christ or there will be no joy, for He is the source of joy. As Henry Altemus has said, "The one great source of Christian joy is Christ." But let us go on, because joy also sustains us in our trials.

The believer can be sustained through all his trials by

the Person of Christ. "That the trial of your faith, being much more precious than of gold that perisheth, though it be tried with fire, might be found unto praise and honour and glory at the appearing of Jesus Christ" (1 Pet. 1:7). Many people rest in false hope, but our hope is in the Person of Christ. He goes with us through the fiery trials which are more precious than gold that perishes. Do you consider your trials and problems more valuable than a hundred bars of gold, at $400 an ounce? Have you thanked God for that trial or problem He sent into your life? First Peter 1:8 goes on to say, "Whom having not seen, ye love; in whom, though now ye see him not, yet believing, ye rejoice with joy unspeakable and full of glory." Remember, the fruit of love comes before the fruit of joy. You cannot have joy until you have love. In his first chapter, James tells of a person whose trial is not a problem to him because he loves the Lord. The term "joy unspeakable" means "glorified joy." It speaks of the glory of Jehovah Himself. He gives us "glorified joy" which sustains us through our trials. No wonder James says, ". . . count it all joy when ye fall into divers temptations" (James 1:2). Paul adds, "In every thing give thanks: for this is the will of God in Christ Jesus concerning you" (1 Thess. 5:18). I came home late one afternoon and decided to take a half hour snooze before supper. As I was enjoying a pleasant dream and anticipating a delicious beef stew dinner, there was a big boom in the kitchen. My wife had noticed a little steam sneaking out of the pressure cooker and thought it was not tight enough. As she tightened it—BOOM—we had wall-to-wall beef stew. She came and stood silently in the room for moment. When I asked what was wrong, and she didn't answer, I went to the kitchen and found the disaster. I asked, "Would you like to go to Burger King tonight?" We learned how to give thanks for our problem and not let our problem overcome us. There was no use crying over spilled beef stew. Are you allowing God to sustain you through your trials? Paul says in Philippians 4:4, "Rejoice in the Lord alway: and again I say, Rejoice." Man is prone to be defeated by his circumstances. We need to see trials as given by God to strengthen us and mold our character. Through them God teaches us what true joy is. We learn to abide in Christ, deepening our roots in His saving grace. Someone has written:

> One with Christ, oh, joy divine!
> I am His and He is mine,
> Oh the wonder of His grace!
> He is my abiding place.
> One with Christ 'til life is o'er,
> One with Christ forever more.

III. The Joy of Surrender for Service

We not only have the joy of salvation and the joy of fellowship but the joy of surrender for service. Joy is the key to effective service. Isaiah 65:14 says, "My servants shall sing for joy of heart." Every pastor, missionary, evangelist, Sunday School teacher, deacon, church officer or church worker needs to see that there is joy in serving Jesus. Can you imagine someone telling another of the joy in Christ if he is unhappy and miserable himself? Many people are ineffective in their service for Christ because they lack joy in their personal lives. It would be better for us to sit and learn how to abide in Christ and cultivate joy before we try to serve the Lord. Psalm 100:2 requires that we "Serve the LORD with gladness." Nehemiah 8:10 says, "The joy of the LORD is your strength."

Joy is the key in soul winning. In 1 Thessalonians 2:19 and 20 Paul shares his own experience, "For what is our hope, or joy, or crown of rejoicing? Are not even ye in the presence of our Lord Jesus Christ at his coming? For ye are our glory and joy." Paul's joy in the second coming of Christ is having led these people to a saving knowledge of Jesus Christ. How joyful he will be on that grand reunion day to see those who, through his preaching of the Word, came to Jesus Christ in Ephesus, Antioch, Philippi, Corinth, Rome and other cities.

What a joyful day it will be to stand in the presence of the Lord and hear someone say, "Thank you for bringing me to Christ."

Joy is also the reward for faithful service. Matthew 25:23 declares, "Well done, good and faithful servant; thou hast been faithful over a few things, I will make thee ruler over many things: enter thou into the joy of thy lord." The real reward given to the faithful believer is joy. Salvation begins with joy and ends in joy.

We retain the possession of our joy by abiding in our Savior's love; by living daily upon His fullness; by resting beneath His shadow; by lovingly obeying His commands; by submissively receiving all His chastening; by joyfully welcoming all His rebukes; by unhesitatingly following all His leadings; by glorifying Him in mercy and in trials, in health and in sickness, in prosperity as well as adversity, until that blessed hour when He will take us home and we will drink from the river of His pleasure and partake of the joys that are at God's right hand forever.

Research Bibliography

DeHaan, Richard. *Happiness Is Not an Accident.* Grand Rapids: Zondervan, 1971.

Edman, V. Raymond. *The Disciplines of Life.* Minneapolis: World Wide Publications, 1948.

Graham, William F. *The Secret of Happiness.* Garden City, NY: Double Day, 1955.

H.W.S. *The Christian's Secret of a Happy Life.* Boston: Williard Tract Repository, 1875.

Jauncey, James H. *Above Ourselves.* Grand Rapids: Zondervan, 1964.

McCormick, William. *Be of Good Cheer.* New York: Longmans, Green & Co., 1930.

Sanders, J. Oswald. *A Spiritual Clinic.* Chicago: Moody Press, 1961.

Questions for Research and Discussion

1. Describe the moment of your salvation and the joy you experienced at that time.
2. If you no longer experience the joy of salvation, determine what caused its loss. How do you plan to restore that joy?
3. What does it mean to experience the presence of God? Is God as real to you as your best friend or just an abstract of theology? How can you bring God into personal fellowship with your life?
4. Examine two or three trials you recently experienced. How did you handle them? How would God want you to have handled them? Use the following chart as a guide.

Trial	What I did wrong in response	How God would have wanted me to respond

5. Make a list of Scripture promises about joy and write down your insights of what they mean to you. Use a concordance.

Chapter 6

The Fruit of the Spirit is

PEACE

A blind Fanny Crosby, at the early age of 8, wrote these words:

> O what a happy soul am I!
> Although I cannot see,
> I am resolved that in this world
> Contented I will be;
> How many blessings I enjoy,
> That other people don't!
> To weep and sigh because I'm blind,
> I cannot and I won't.

Looking through one hymnbook, I counted twenty-three of her hymns. God did something in her life because she was willing to rest content in His will for her life. Many people would become anxious and troubled over such a trial, but she found the fruit of peace ruling her heart. The Bible deals with God's peace in several ways.

I. Peace with God

The peace by which God provides salvation is called "peace *with* God." Another term, the "peace *of* God," is the peace He provides by His grace for daily Christian living. An unsaved person cannot know the peace of God until he experiences peace with God. Therefore, the sinner is without peace. Isaiah 57:20 and 21 declare, "The wicked are like the troubled sea, when it cannot rest, whose waters cast up mire and dirt. There is no peace, saith my God, to the wicked." I had the privilege of growing up along the New England coastline just five miles from the ocean. When there was a storm brewing out to sea, the waves would be tossed against the rocks. It was thrilling to drive along the back roads that few knew about by the ocean and just watch the raging, troubled sea. Yet, it is not so thrilling that this is how the Bible describes the life of the sinner outside of Jesus Christ. He is like the troubled sea casting up mire and dirt. You learn not to go swimming after a storm because of the filthy, churned-up water. We were camping along Florida's Gulf Coast some years ago and after settling at our campsite, we went to the beach and found it so dirty and slimy that we could not swim. At first appearance it looked inviting, but in reality it was unclean. The Bible says that is the same problem with the sinner. He may look fine on the outside, but inside he is full of all uncleanness. Romans 3:17 says, "The way of peace have they not known."

Have you ever wondered why there are so many problems in the world? We talk about peace in the Middle East, with China, Russia and in countries with revolutions, but there is no peace. The reason is that unsaved hearts will never find peace apart from Christ.

A native on Malabar sought peace from the local witch doctor. The witch doctor told him he could have peace if he put six inch-long spikes through the bottom of his sandals facing up and walked 480 miles to another city. The man said, "If that will give me peace, I'll do it." The witch doctor then said, "You are not to stop unless you become faint through bleeding. Once you are healed you are to go on. When you get to the end, you will have peace." The man had journeyed several days when he could take no more pain. The torture and loss of blood was so great that he sank down beside a tree outside a little mission station. The missionary was teaching the Word of God to the people in the mission compound. He was preaching God's truth in 1 John 1:7, ". . . the blood of Jesus Christ his Son cleanseth us from all sin." The man under the tree got up, ran to the missionary and said, "That's what I've been looking for." He threw his nail-spiked sandals away and said, "I don't need these anymore. I have found true peace in Jesus Christ." There is no peace apart from Christ, Who is our source of peace. Isaiah 53:5 says, ". . . the chastisement of our peace was upon him; and with his stripes we are healed."

Ephesians 2 also acknowledges Christ as our source of peace. "But now in Christ Jesus ye who sometimes were far off are made nigh by the blood of Christ. For he is our peace, . . ." (Eph. 2:13, 14). In this world of trial, trouble, sin and turmoil, there is One Who can provide, not a superficial peace, but true, inward, abiding peace with God.

We who once were God's enemies now have peace with God through the appropriation of faith. Romans 5:1 declares, "Therefore being justified by faith, we have peace with God through our Lord Jesus Christ." How do we obtain peace with God? We appropriate it by faith. Faith is taking for ourselves what God has done at Calvary through the shed blood of Christ. The result is justification. Justification is a legal word. God legally acts as a Judge to take my sin and place it upon Christ at Calvary. He then takes the righteousness of Christ and places it upon me. Then, when He looks at my life, He no longer sees me as a sinner but as righteous through Christ. He declares me justified. The enmity with God is removed and peace with God can be claimed.

At the annual meeting of the British and Foreign Bible Society in 1907, a Canadian missionary shared an illustration of how God brought peace to many troubled hearts. The Mackenzie River runs two thousand miles from Edmonton to the Arctic Ocean. Every three hundred miles along the river, there was a trading post with a large stockade for protection. Each trading post had a mission attached to it. The missionaries were so effective in winning people to Christ that the stockade was torn down for firewood. The enemies had been won to Christ and the wall of partition had been taken away. God had provided peace through His Son.

Peace with God is the provision of Christ for a troubled sinner. Have you found that peace? Thomas Chisholm expressed it:

> I yet were in my sins,
> Mind and conscience unrelieved,
> No God, no hope, sweet pardon, rest,
> Unless I had believed.
>
> But now I have believed!
> And God's glory I have seen!
> His great salvation shown to me,
> My sinful heart made clean.

II. Peace of God

Once we have peace with God and are made members of God's family, God wants to supply another type of peace for us—the peace of God. Christ is the provider of the peace of God for the believer. In John 14:27 He said, "Peace I leave with you, my peace I give unto you: not as the world giveth, give I unto you. Let not your heart be troubled, neither let it be afraid." When the disciples heard that Christ was going to die and leave them, they were troubled and anxious. Their minds could not comprehend it. Have you ever come to the place where mentally you could not figure out a solution to a problem or emotionally could not deal with it? Have you ever lacked the willpower to struggle with a trial? In those very moments God wants to provide His peace for the believer.

Inside the old castles of Europe, one often finds deep wells which were built for the time of seige by the enemy. If the inhabitants of the castle were dependent on some outside stream or river they would be in trouble, for it could be kept from their access by damming or polluting it. So the inhabitants of the castle dug a well deep enough so they would have an inside source of water. That is similar to the peace of God for the believer. We may have troubles without, but in the Person of Christ we have an everlasting supply of the Peace of God. The peace of God is well described in Philippians 4:7, "And the peace of God, which passeth all understanding, shall keep your hearts and minds through Christ Jesus."

What are the means of retaining the peace of God within our lives? How can we have this inside source of peace that overcomes anxiety and frustration? There are five major means of retaining the peace of God:

1. Faith—Romans 15:13

"Now the God of hope fill you with all joy and peace in believing. . . ." In the act of habitually believing the promises of the Word of God, the Spirit of God provides peace. We are not to walk by sight but by faith. We walk by faith by wearing the eyeglasses of the Word of God. We will be in trouble if we trust the flesh and human wisdom. We must by faith surrender to the Holy Spirit and God's Word if there is to be joy and peace in believing. Many people who do not recognize faith as the inward source of the peace of God will become hopeless and discouraged. If they allow discouragement to continue long enough, it will lead to doubt and despair. Faith is the first resource for keeping the peace of God.

2. The Scriptures—Psalm 119:165

"Great peace have they which love thy law. . . ." How much do you love the Word of God? How much of the Scripture have you committed to memory? I once gave myself a little test in this area. I lived about a mile and a half from church and decided as I walked that distance to move only while quoting the Scriptures from memory. I started in Genesis with all the verses I could remember, reciting them mentally as I walked. I was quoting from Revelation when I arrived at church. Another half mile and I would have been in trouble. A doctor friend in New York City memorized Scripture while he jogged ten miles each day. If we are to have God's peace we must know God's Word.

3. Spiritual (Biblical) thinking—Romans 8:6

"To be carnally minded is death; but to be spiritually minded is life and peace." Some people think that to be spiritually minded you must have a mystical experience with God. But the key to being spiritually minded is to be Scripturally oriented. The more we know and practice the Word of God, the more we think Biblically. Since the Spirit of God is the author of the Word, to be spiritually minded is to know the Word of God. We must allow the Spirit to teach us, direct us, and give us discernment. The more we operate our thinking processes Scripturally, the more spiritually minded we will be. Every problem, decision, trial and heartache must be related to the Word of God. The next time you face a problem ask, What does God's Word say about this problem? God's Word has the answer and it will provide peace.

4. Communion with God—Numbers 6:26

"The LORD lift up his countenance upon thee, and give thee peace." What is meant by "countenance"? A person's countenance is seen in his facial expressions and eyes. When the Lord lifts up His countenance upon us to give us peace, we need to be "eye to eye" with Him. That is communion, fellowship or walking with God. God spoke to Moses face to face. God has provided in the Bible the greatest miracle outside of the finished work of Christ on Calvary. He has given to us face to face contact with Himself. Moses had only a little knowledge of God, but we have the completed Scripture. When we meditate upon the Scriptures we come face to face with the Holy God of Heaven and can walk in communion with Him. The result is that we will retain peace.

5. Prayer—Philippians 4:6, 7

"Be careful [anxious] for nothing; but in every thing by prayer and supplication with thanksgiving let your requests be made known unto God. And the peace of God, which passeth all understanding, shall keep your hearts and minds through Christ Jesus." The peace of God comes when by faith we appropriate it in prayer and submit to His will. God gives peace for the work of sanctification. He intends to provide emotional and mental stability for the believer. Colossians 3:15 shows that peace is to judge all other emotions, "And let the peace of God rule in your hearts, to the which also ye are called in one body; and be ye thankful." The Greek word "rule" means "to umpire." The peace of God is to umpire our final decisions. It is the final authority in our lives. If you are walking with God in prayer He will give you peace.

R. A. Torrey once encountered a time of sudden distress and unrest of soul because his prayers were not being answered. He recognized the absence of peace and asked the Lord to show him by the Scriptures what was wrong. After he read the Word of God over the next few days, God zeroed in on some areas of his life. After he confessed and forsook them, peace returned, prayers were answered and joy was restored in his life.

III. Peace with Others

Peace with God relates to salvation. The peace of God deals with sanctification. Another part of the peace of God is to have peace with others. The Bible commands us to be at peace with other individuals: ". . . Have peace one with another" (Mark 9:50); ". . . live peaceably with all men" (Rom. 12:18); ". . . be at peace among yourselves" (1 Thess. 5:13). The Bible teaches us that God's peace must not only pass all understanding but all misunderstanding. People who growl and bark at each other deserve to live a dog's life. They have an absence of peace. The Bible commands us to "follow peace with all men" (Heb. 12:14). A person who is not courteous fails to exhibit the peace of God and shows a lack of spirituality. Second Corinthians 13:11 says, ". . . be of one mind, live in peace. . . ." It has been said that sour grapes have turned over a lot of apple carts. We need to live with the peace of God ruling our lives. First Corinthians 14:33 states, "God is not the author of confusion, but of peace, as in all churches of the saints." A Bible-believing church should possess an atmosphere of peace, where everyone loves one another and is experiencing the joy of Christ. Those who have inward peace will express it outwardly to others. James concludes chapter 3 this way: "For where envying and strife is, there is confusion and every evil work. But the wisdom that is from above is first pure, then peaceable, gentle, and easy to be intreated, full of mercy and good fruits, without partiality, and without hypocrisy. And the fruit of righteousness is sown in peace of them that make peace" (James 3:16–18). Romans 14:19 demands, "Let us therefore follow after the things which make for peace, and things wherewith one may edify another." The way we build up other Christians is through exhibiting the fruit of the Spirit which is peace.

Research Bibliography

Baxter, Richard. *The Saints' Everlasting Rest.* London: The Epworth Press, 1962.

Brandt, Henry. *The Struggle for Peace.* Wheaton, IL: Scripture Press Publications, 1969.

Crabb, Lawrence, Jr. *Effective Biblical Counseling.* Grand Rapids: Zondervan, 1979.

Gage, Robert. *Our Life in Christ—The Peace of God.* Grand Rapids: Sword & Shield Ministries, 1978.

Graham, William F. *Peace With God.* Garden City, NY: Doubleday, 1953.

Mobbs, Bernard. *Our Rebel Emotions.* New York: Seabury Press, 1970.

Questions for Research and Discussion

1. Have you experienced peace *with* God through salvation? Discuss how Christ is the source of this peace. If you have not received Christ as your personal Savior, is there any reason you cannot do so now? If you have, seek to share your testimony with two people this week.
2. Discuss how Christ provides the inward peace *of* God for the believer. Using the following chart, what areas do you need to cultivate to retain this peace? How do you plan to do it?

Means of retaining the peace of God	How do I score? (check one) Exc.	Vy. Gd.	Good	Fair	Poor	Vy. Pr.	How can I improve?
1. Faith							
2. Scripture							
3. Spiritual (Biblical) Thinking							
4. Communion with God							
5. Prayer							

3. Discuss how inward peace (according to Col. 3:15) acts as an umpire over our emotions.
4. If you are experiencing conflict with some individual, study the verses relating to our peace with others. Develop plans for resolving this conflict.
5. Study Philippians 4 to see how Paul experienced the peace of God. Using verse 8 and the following chart as a guide, list several items under each area about which we are to develop the habit of meditation.

Area of Meditation	**List 3 items that relate to this characteristic**		
Things that are:	**1**	**2**	**3**
1. True			
2. Honest			
3. Just			
4. Pure			
5. Lovely			
6. Of good report			
7. Virtuous			
8. Praise-worthy			

Chapter 7

The Fruit of the Spirit is

LONGSUFFERING

The parable of persistence is a story of two frogs who lived in a little pond outside a big city. They had enjoyed the pond for many months. One day a farmer, with several jugs of milk on his wagon, came by the pond on his way to the big city to sell his milk. He decided that he could get more revenue if he had more milk, so he took a bucket, filled it with water and added it to the milk jugs. Unknowingly, in one bucket he had also picked up the two frogs. The frogs soon found themselves bouncing around in a jug of milk on their way to the city. The frogs realized their danger and kicked vigorously to keep their heads above the milk. After a while, one of the frogs became disheartened and said, "Let's give up, go to the bottom and end it all; it's no use." The other frog optimistically replied, "Let's keep kicking as long as we can and see what happens; maybe things will change."

So one frog disappeared under the surface and was never seen again. The other little frog paddled as hard as he could. Finally the farmer arrived in the city and took the jugs of milk into the store. When he opened the jug, he was amazed to see the frog sitting comfortably on a lump of butter. The moral of the parable of persistence is, "Never give up; keep paddling;

keep kicking." Many Christians would rather give up than cultivate the fruit of the Spirit which is longsuffering.

What is longsuffering? Vine defines longsuffering as "that quality of self-restraint in the face of provocation which does not hastily retaliate or promptly punish; it is the opposite of anger and is associated with mercy. . . ."[1] Longsuffering and patience are cousins. Longsuffering relates to people, patience to circumstances. We are to be longsuffering with people and patient with our circumstances. Actually, longsuffering is love in action. In 1 Corinthians 13, one characteristic of God's love is longsuffering. The word in Hebrew means "long-fused," meaning one does not easily blow up, become angry or upset.

I. God's Longsuffering

To understand longsuffering, we need to examine its first mention in the Scripture, where it is seen as an attribute of God. Exodus 34:5–7 says:

> And the LORD descended in the cloud, and stood with him there, and proclaimed the name of the LORD. And the LORD passed by before him, and proclaimed, The LORD, The LORD God, merciful and gracious, longsuffering, and abundant in goodness and truth, Keeping mercy for thousands, forgiving iniquity and transgression and sin, and that will by no means clear the guilty; visiting the iniquity of the fathers upon the children, and upon the children's children, unto the third and to the fourth generation.

If we look at the context, we find that while Moses was on the mountain with the Lord, the Israelites made a golden calf to worship. When Moses saw Israel dancing before the golden calf in their idolatrous worship, he broke the tables of the law to symbolize the fact that Israel had broken the commandments of God. While Moses is wondering what to do with these rebellious Jews, God says, "I want to tell you something about myself. I am the Lord God, merciful and gracious, longsuffering, abundant in goodness and truth." As a God of justice, He decrees that sin must be punished. But as a God of love, He presents this characteristic or attribute of longsuffering. The second use of the term longsuffering is in Numbers 14:17-20:

> And now, I beseech thee, let the power of my Lord be great, according as thou hast spoken, saying, The LORD is longsuffering, and of great mercy, forgiving iniquity and transgression, and by no means clearing the guilty, visiting the iniquity of the fathers upon the children unto the third and fourth generation. Pardon, I beseech thee, the iniquity of this people according unto the greatness of thy mercy, and as thou hast forgiven this people, from Egypt even until now. And the LORD said, I have pardoned according to thy word.

Again Moses is talking to the Lord about the children of Israel. What have they done this time? The twelve spies had returned and given their reports. Caleb and Joshua by faith had declared, "We ought to go in and win the battle." The others pessimistically said, "The people are too big for us. We can't tackle such problems. There are too many difficulties. We'll be killed." The children of Israel listened to the evil report. God was ready to bring judgment, but Moses pleaded in prayer before the Lord, reminding Him that He was a God of compassion and longsuffering. God then responded, "I have pardoned according to thy word." God is longsuffering.

God's longsuffering is related to His other attributes. Psalm 86:15 says, "But thou, O Lord, art a God full of compassion, and gracious, longsuffering, and plenteous in mercy and truth." Longsuffering is particularly related to the subject of salvation. In Romans 2:4, Paul tells of God's longsuffering, "Or despisest thou the riches of his goodness and forbearance and longsuffering; not knowing that the goodness of God leadeth thee to repentance?" God's longsuffering puts up with sinful men. Someone asks, "Why does a God of love allow all the sin, hunger and wars in today's world?" He does because He is a God of longsuffering. If He did not have this attribute, He would immediately destroy sin and sinners. But He desires to make people with sin natures into people with new natures. Peter talks of God's longsuffering in salvation. "The Lord is not slack concerning his promise, as some men count slackness; but is longsuffering to us-ward, not willing that any should perish, but that all should come to repentance" (2 Pet. 3:9). Have you ever wondered why God holds back the Rapture? He is a God of longsuffering, not willing that any should perish but that all would repent. When the last elect person in the Church Age has come to repentance, Christ will come for the Church. Second Peter 3:15 says, "And account that the longsuffering of our Lord is salvation. . . ." God is desirous that the unsaved know the truth about salvation, come to repentance and have eternal life through Christ.

Paul's personal testimony to Timothy speaks of this longsuffering of God:

> This is a faithful saying, and worthy of all acceptation, that Christ Jesus came into the world to save sinners; of whom I am chief. Howbeit for this cause I obtained mercy, that in me first Jesus Christ might shew forth all longsuffering, for a pattern to them which should hereafter believe on him to life everlasting (1 Tim. 1:15, 16).

Paul had been a renegade, a Pharisee persecuting the church, an arrogant, Christ-defying individual. Paul saw his own salvation as the result of God's longsuffering. The hymnwriter knew something of God's longsuffering when he wrote:

> O love that will not let me go,
>   I rest my weary soul in Thee;
> I give Thee back the life I owe,
>   That in Thine ocean depths its flow,
> May richer, fuller be.

II. The Spiritual Character of Longsuffering

Notice the spiritual character of longsuffering as it relates to the fruit of the Spirit. Remember, there are nine aspects of the fruit of the Spirit, not nine fruits. It is one fruit displayed in nine different ways. A person either has all nine or none. Where does longsuffering belong in these nine aspects?

Longsuffering is a result of love, joy and peace. If I have love, joy and peace, I will have longsuffering. If I do not have longsuffering, it is because I have no love, joy or peace.

Longsuffering is the cause of gentleness and goodness. Longsuffering will make a person gentle. A husband or a wife who pleads with the Lord for longsuffering toward a mate will cultivate a disposition of gentleness and goodness.

Longsuffering, gentleness and goodness then become the foundation of faith, meekness and self-control. One cannot control his temper until he has asked God for longsuffering. When you get longsuffering, you will have self-control.

Longsuffering's Relationship to the Fruit of the Spirit

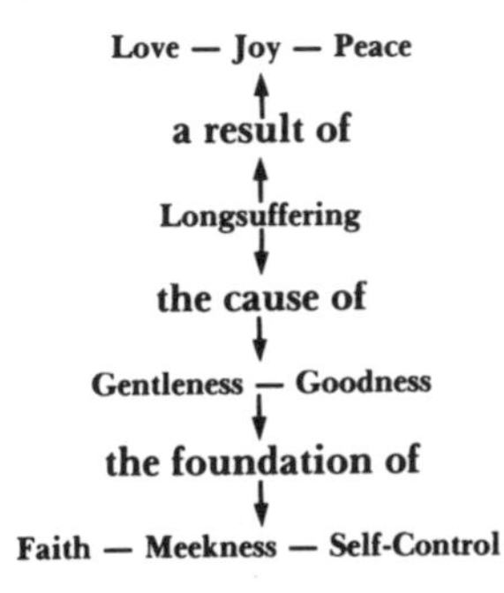

Longsuffering is also related to Biblical preaching and ministry. In 2 Timothy 4:2, Paul tells Timothy the importance of longsuffering. "Preach the word; be instant in season, out of season; reprove, rebuke, exhort with all longsuffering and doctrine." Oh, how preachers love to hear those words, "reprove, rebuke, exhort." We say, "I'm going to do that by teaching good doctrine." But God says there is something else involved: longsuffering.

When beginning my first pastorate, I decided to plan

an entire year of preaching that would take everybody step by step through the whole Bible so they would know everything. That was unrealistic optimism. At the end of the year, on a Wednesday night, we had a question and answer time. I found that the things I had preached all year had not been understood. I learned the important lesson of teaching things over and over again. If it does not take hold the first time, preach it again. We must preach with longsuffering. Preaching the Word of God changes lives. Paul approved himself as a minister, "by pureness, by knowledge, by longsuffering, by kindness, by the Holy [Spirit], by love unfeigned" (2 Cor. 6:6).

III. The Practical Application of Longsuffering

In Ephesians 4:2 and 3, Paul relates longsuffering to the Church. The Church will maintain spiritual unity when longsuffering is exercised. "With all lowliness and meekness, with longsuffering, forbearing one another in love; Endeavoring to keep the unity of the Spirit in the bond of peace." Spiritual unity among believers results as we exercise longsuffering toward one another. Such application of longsuffering is putting love into action within our lives. If someone at church rubs us the wrong way, instead of seeking another church we should pray, "Lord, thank You for that irritation. Help me to be an instrument of love to that individual. Help me to have longsuffering." Two hundred years before Christ, Plautus said, "Patience is the best remedy for every trouble." The Bible agrees; longsuffering is the best remedy for every problem we face with other individuals.

Longsuffering is also the means of spiritual power and joy. In Colossians 1:11 Paul said, "Strengthened with all might, according to his glorious power, unto all patience and longsuffering with joyfulness." If we practice longsuffering in our lives we will experience joy. The fruit of the Spirit is so interrelated that you cannot separate one from the other. Longsuffering, spiritual power and joy can encompass anything.

When a person exercises longsuffering, he can conquer problems that normally would defeat him.

Longsuffering is also the means of spiritual maturity. Read Colossians 3:12, "Put on therefore, as the elect of God, holy and beloved, bowels of mercies, kindness, humbleness of mind, meekness, longsuffering." How do I have longsuffering? "Forbearing one another, and forgiving one another . . ." (v. 13). The word "forbearing" literally means to restrain from provoking. Do not do something that is going to purposely upset someone else. "If any man have a quarrel [or a disagreement] against any: even as Christ forgave you, so also do ye. And above all these things put on [love], which is the bond of perfectness" (vv. 13, 14). The word "perfect" means spiritually mature. Longsuffering will lead us to become mature, spiritual individuals who will honor and glorify God.

It is easy to find reasons why other people should be patient but very difficult for us to be patient. Someone has said, "There are times when God asks nothing of His children, except silence, patience and tears." That is longsuffering. Are you willing to be silent? Are you willing to suffer? Remember, love in action has an appropriate name—longsuffering. Somehow Christians have the idea that they should always be happy and never have to suffer or endure anything. Love is quite the opposite. Love suffers. Think how annoying sin is to the holiness of God. God could with His omnipotent power wipe out every sinner on the face of the earth in a moment. But He does not because He is longsuffering. Are we willing to cultivate such longsuffering in our lives?

Research Bibliography

Dobson, James. *Emotions, Can You Trust Them?* Ventura, CA: Regal Books, 1980.

Getz, Gene A. *The Measure of a Church.* Glendale, CA: Regal Books, 1976.

LaHaye, Tim. *Anger is a Choice.* Grand Rapids: Zondervan, 1982.

MacArthur, John, Jr. *The Church, the Body of Christ.* Grand Rapids: Zondervan, 1978.

Peace, Richard. *Learning to Love People.* Grand Rapids: Zondervan, 1968.

Schaeffer, Frances A. *True Spirituality.* Wheaton, IL: Tyndale House, 1973.

Scroggie, W. G. *The Love Life (1 Corinthians 13).* Grand Rapids: Kregel, 1980.

Questions for Research and Discussion

1. What is longsuffering? How does it relate to patience?
2. Discuss God's longsuffering and how it provides an example to us. How is God longsuffering to the unsaved? How is He longsuffering toward believers? How is He longsuffering to you?
3. How does longsuffering relate to the other aspects of the fruit of the Spirit? Fill in the following:

   Longsuffering is the result of ___________ , ___________ and ___________ .

   Longsuffering is the cause of _________ and _________ .

   Longsuffering is the foundation of ________ , ________ and ______________ .

4. Discuss how longsuffering can be practically applied to:
   a. the spiritual unity of the church
   b. our personal spiritual power and joy
   c. our own spiritual maturity
5. List several people, circumstances or things that irritate you or may cause you to become angry, upset or even bitter. Using our study of the fruit of longsuffering, write out the reaction God wants you to have.

Problem	How God wants me to react with longsuffering
1.	
2.	
3.	

Chapter 8

The Fruit of the Spirit is

GENTLENESS

Many people blow situations and ruin friendships because they do not use the fruit of the Spirit which is gentleness when dealing with others. We need gentleness in our marriages, homes, friendships and churches. James Hamilton said, "True gentleness is love in society, holding intercourse with those around it. It is consideration, it is tenderness in feeling, it is promptness of sympathy, it is love in all its depths and delicacy. It is everything included in that matchless grace called the gentleness of Christ."[1] To be gentle means to be equitable, fair and moderate. It is being forbearing instead of insisting on the letter of the law. Gentleness looks with reason at all the facts before passing judgment. The person who shows gentleness acts humanely toward other people. This fruit of the Spirit is vitally needed in our day.

People who visit our Bible-believing churches should see Christians exercising this fruit of the Spirit by putting love into action. Remember, love is the first aspect of the fruit of the Spirit and controls all others that follow. In gentleness, love is put into action in our relationship to others. How much do we love others? In 1 John 4:7 John says, in effect, "We show our love to God by loving our brother in Christ." James asks us to show faith by works in James chapter 2. Gentleness is this exercising of love and faith.

I. The Example of Christ

The Lord Jesus Christ is our best example of gentleness. Isaiah's prophecy of the Messiah was that He would gently lead (Isa. 40:11). Paul saw this characteristic in Christ when he said, "I . . . beseech you by the meekness and gentleness of Christ. . ." (2 Cor. 10:1). Gentleness in the disposition and character of Christ was best seen in His suffering for us. First Peter 2:21-25 reminds us:

> For even hereunto were ye called: because Christ also suffered for us, leaving us an example, that ye should follow his steps: Who did no sin, neither was guile found in his mouth: Who, when he was reviled, reviled not again; when he suffered, he threatened not; but committed himself to him that judgeth righteously: Who his own self bare our sins in his own body on the tree, that we, being dead to sins, should live unto righteousness: by whose stripes ye were healed. For ye were as sheep going astray; but are now returned unto the Shepherd and Bishop of your souls.

Our wonderful Shepherd went to Calvary to take the judgment of hell that we deserved. He suffered and died in our place that we might have eternal life. When Christ suffered for us on the cross, He did not say, "I don't want to do this." When He was rebuked, mocked and scorned, He did not say, "I don't like this." That is what we too often say when we go through trials. We cry out, "Lord, I don't want this in my life. This burden is too heavy, this problem too great for me to solve. I can't do it. I can't take the pressure." The Lord was not that way when He suffered for us; He committed Himself to His Father. In doing so He shared with us the great example of the fruit of gentleness. In our problems, difficulties, afflictions and trials, we need to commit ourselves into God's hand and let Him take over.

A settler in South Africa saw a native on his property and charged him with trying to steal some of his cattle. After declaring him guilty without a chance to explain, the settler had a few servants hold the native's arm against a tree and chop off his hand. Sometime later, the settler got lost in the bush country. He came across a little hut and asked permission to stay the night. In the morning when the settler awoke, he noticed his host was without a hand. The home in which he was being so graciously entertained belonged to the man whose hand he had chopped off! He fearfully asked, "Are you going to take my life?" The native replied, "Sir, I'm a Christian. I thought of retaliation but knew that my Lord would not want me to do so. I could not do that, because my Lord loves me and I love you, though you were wrong in taking my hand. I will do you no harm." That African was expressing the fruit of the Spirit which is gentleness. Do we display gentleness in our lives as we face problems, difficulties and suffering?

II. The Result of Inner Contentment

The fruit of gentleness is really the result of inward contentment. Many people are not gentle outwardly because they are in turmoil inside. Gentleness is a result of being inwardly right with God. Second Samuel 22:36 and Psalm 18:35 say, "Thou hast also given me the shield of thy salvation: . . . and thy gentleness hath made me great." People often look for greatness and power, yet these come through gentleness. The person who cultivates this characteristic will be great. Francis deSales said, "Nothing is so strong as gentleness, nothing so gentle as real strength."[2] We need to learn to bear injuries and annoying events meekly, patiently and prayerfully with self-control. Gentleness expresses the wisdom described in James 3:17 and 18:

> But the wisdom that is from above is first pure, then peaceable, gentle, and easy to be intreated, full of mercy and good fruits,

> without partiality, and without hypocrisy. And the fruit of righteousness is sown in peace of them that make peace.

Gentleness has its origin in true wisdom. It is cultivated within our minds by the ability to think Biblically, that is, the way God wants us to think.

As we face difficulties and problems, gentleness will produce peace and contentment within our lives. Paul declares, "But godliness with contentment is great gain" (1 Tim. 6:6). Holiness of living with inner contentment is the goal of the Christian life. Godliness with contentment is described in 1 Timothy 6:8, "And having food and raiment let us be therewith content." If we have cultivated gentleness in order to produce contentment, we will be satisfied with the things we have. We will seek first the kingdom of God and His righteousness, knowing all these things will be added to us. Hebrews 13:5 says, ". . . be content with such things as ye have. . . ." Inner contentment results from outer gentleness. Someone has said, "The contented man is never poor, the discontented never rich." A person can have all the wealth of the world, but without inward spiritual contentment, there will be no true happiness.

Paul says, "Not that I speak in respect of want: for I have learned, in whatsoever state I am, therewith to be content" (Phil. 4:11). Paul experienced peace in all situations, problems and trials because he was contented. Total surrender to Christ allows the Spirit of God to give inward peace and outward gentleness.

III. The Disposition of Peace

Since gentleness is the result of inner contentment in the believer's life, how is it to be displayed? Remember, gentleness is love in action, bringing joy and contentment to the Christian's life through a disposition of peace. Gentleness is therefore an attitude of love and sacrifice. Paul expresses his own attitude among fellow believers in this way:

> But we were gentle among you, even as a nurse cherisheth her

> children: So being affectionately desirous of you, we were willing to have imparted unto you, not the gospel of God only, but also our own souls, because ye were dear unto us (1 Thess. 2:7, 8).

How close are we to our Christian friends? One thing that should happen within a local church is the developing of love for one another. We are to bear burdens, pray for each other and display our love and friendship. We are to edify one another, not only by teaching the truths of the Word, but by undergirding people in their problems and difficulties. What a tremendous thing to know that, as you enter the hospital, there are people praying for you. If you face a crisis on your job or lose a loved one in death, there are Christian friends praying for you.

We are told in Titus 3:2 to be ". . . gentle, showing all meekness unto all men." Gentleness displays itself in our attitudes, temper, aims and desires. The gentle Christian is mild, calm, quiet, even and temperate. He will not be hasty in judgment, exorbitant in ambition, overbearing, proud or oppressive, for these are contrary to true gentleness.

We are to have gentleness in suffering for Christ. First Peter 2:18 and 19 say, "Servants, be subject to your masters with all fear; not only to the good and gentle, but also to the froward. For this is thankworthy, if a man for conscience toward God endure grief, suffering wrongfully." It is easy to respond to people who are nice to us. But how do we react to those who are unkind, to those who may mock our faith in Christ? We need to minister to them by displaying the gentle disposition of peace.

We need gentleness also in correcting others. Paul advises us how to correct the fault of a wife, husband, friend or neighbor in 2 Timothy 2:23-26:

> But foolish and unlearned questions avoid, knowing that they do gender strifes. And the servant of the Lord must not strive; but be gentle unto all men, apt to teach, patient, In meekness

instructing those that oppose themselves; if God peradventure will give them repentance to the acknowledging of the truth; And that they may recover themselves out of the snare of the devil, who are taken captive by him at his will.

Real edification and correction are accomplished by gently teaching with patience, meekness and humility. We need to cultivate this Biblical approach to problems. Usually we approach problems by exploding rather than by gentle and patient teaching. God will help us learn to use the fruit of gentleness in correcting others as we are careful to speak in soft, tender, kind and loving ways. Even when we have an occasion to rebuke, we must be careful to do it with kindness. The effect will be incalculably better.

A backslider, well known to the evangelist, slipped into the back of the auditorium where the evangelist was speaking. He noticed the preacher had seen him and, fearing rebuke for his backslidden condition, left during the closing prayer. A few days later he unexpectedly met the preacher. The man thought to himself, "Here it comes; he's going to call me a wicked backslider!" But the evangelist looked at him and said gently and calmly, "God loves you, Christ loves you and I love you." The backslider stood there, speechless. He had already planned his defense for the rebuke but did not know how to respond to this gentleness. Tears streamed down his face and repentance took over his heart. The gentleness of Christ arrested his attention and brought his soul back to the place of faithfulness with God.

Gentleness involves forbearance. The word for forbearance is the same Greek word as moderation found in Philippians 4:5, "Let your moderation be known unto all men. The Lord is at hand." Since God is right by my side I am to display forbearance. Forbearance is knowing when to bend. I remember seeing a sign in someone's office that said, "A good leader knows the rules. A great leader knows when to bend the rules." Since the Lord is with us, we ought to judge things from His perspective. Forbearance puts our love into action by displaying gentleness. Spurgeon said, "Cultivate forbearance till your heart yields a fine crop. Pray for a short memory as to all unkindness."[3] Robert South, the poet, wrote: "It is a noble and great thing to cover the blemishes and excuse the failings of a friend; to draw a curtain before his stains and to display his perfection; to bury his weakness in silence, but to proclaim his virtues on the housetop."[4] Love covers a multitude of sins, failures and mistakes. It is that type of love that is displayed in the fruit of the Spirit which is gentleness.

There was a pastor who, although very talented and eloquent, lacked sympathy and compassion in dealing with people and their problems. Some people excused him, saying he was too intellectual to be sympathetic to their trials. God dealt with that man the day his baby died and his wife came to the very edge of death. His heart was broken as he turned his life over to God. He became tender, sympathetic, considerate, merciful and compassionate. God cultivated through his great tragedy the fruit of the Spirit which is gentleness. What must God bring into your life and mine to cultivate gentleness?

Research Bibliography

Bunyan, John. *Christian Behavior or, How to Walk So As to Please God.* Swengel, PA: Bible Truth Depot, 1962.

Chafer, Lewis S. *He That Is Spiritual.* Philadelphia: Sunday School Times Co., 1922.

Dale, R. W. *Laws of Christ for Common Life.* London: Hodder and Stoughton, 1911.

Kuyper, Abraham. *The Practice of Godliness.* Grand Rapids: Baker Book House, 1977.

Sanders, John Oswald. *On to Maturity.* Chicago: Moody Press, 1962.

Questions for Research and Discussion

1. What is gentleness? How is it manifested as an example through the Person of Christ?

2. Since gentleness results from inner contentment, list the situations in your life that cause discontent. Next, seek to find the source of discontent and seek to apply this aspect of spiritual fruit as the solution.

	Area of discontent	**Why am I discontent?**	**What is the solution?**
1.			
2.			
3.			
4.			

3. How does this spiritual fruit apply to the way we respond to suffering and trials?
4. Study 2 Timothy 2:20–26. Make a list of ways you can use gentleness in correcting problems in others' lives.

a.

b.

c.

d.

e.

f.

g.

5. How have you responded in the past to acts of unkindness by others? How can you respond differently in the future by cultivating the fruit of gentleness?

How did I respond wrongly?	**What fruit was needed for a right response?**	**How can I cultivate it?**
1.		
2.		
3.		
4.		

Chapter 9

The Fruit of the Spirit is

GOODNESS

A little boy who went to the country fair watched with amazement as a man released a big group of balloons into the air. The boy turned to his father and asked, "How come the red balloon went higher than the yellow balloon?" His father replied, "It's not the color on the outside but what's inside the balloon that made it go higher." So it is with us; what is on the inside affects progress in our spiritual lives. Gentleness inside will produce goodness outside. Gentleness is a good disposition, while goodness is good action in the life of the believer. The word "goodness" signifies the virtuousness of the righteous individual. It is used of those who have been made righteous in the Lord Jesus Christ. The root word means to be upright in character and constitution and beneficial in effect. A study of the Saxon term for deity shows that "God" was an abbreviation of the word "good" and literally meant "the Good One."

I. The Holiness of God

Goodness is the attribute of God that particularly centers around His holiness. God's central characteristic is holiness. If we are to understand the fruit of goodness, we must understand the essential matter of God's holiness. Goodness is characteristic of Deity. God is good because He is holy. Exodus 34:6 speaks of, ". . . The LORD God, merciful and gracious, longsuffering, and abundant in goodness and truth." Zechariah 9:17 declares, "How great is his goodness. . . ." Because God is great, people will seek after Him. Since God is good, He will be found by people. It is the nature of a holy, sovereign God to reveal Himself. He has revealed Himself in the things He has created, which is why people worship the things He has created rather than the Creator Himself. Since God is seen in His creation, man is without excuse. Sociologists have yet to find a culture where people do not have some form of deity. Man universally seeks for God and His truth, but because of depravity he often misses the truth and devises his own way, which leads to destruction.

This good God has revealed Himself not only in His creation but also in the Bible. All we need to know of God is found in the confines of inspired Scripture. Since faith comes by hearing the Word of God, we must heed its message if we are to be accepted by Him. No man can logically understand or diagnose God in a test tube. The Soviet astronauts could not find God in space because they were not looking for Him.

Consider how God has revealed His goodness in the Psalms:

Psalm 23:6—Surely goodness and mercy shall follow me all the days of my life.
Psalm 33:5—. . . the earth is full of the goodness of the LORD.
Psalm 52:1—. . . the goodness of God endureth continually.
Psalm 65:11—Thou crownest the year with thy goodness. . . .
Psalm 107:8—Oh that men would praise the LORD for his goodness, and for his wonderful works to the children of men.
Psalm 107:9 —He . . . filleth the hungry soul with goodness.

God uses His goodness as a means of drawing us to repentance and faith in Christ. In showing the sinfulness of man Romans 2:4 states, "Or despisest thou the riches of his goodness and forbearance and longsuffering; not knowing that the goodness of God leadeth thee to repentance?" God, by His longsuffering and goodness, delays His judgment against wickedness so that man may repent.

God's goodness and holiness is the pathway to true repentance. It is through the holiness of God that we begin to realize how wicked we really are. Once we have seen His holiness, His goodness leads us to repent. Only faith in Christ's sacrificial work at Calvary will make us holy and acceptable to God. We have to be made good before we can do good. We must be justified by faith before we can please God. After we are justified, good works begin.

II. The Sanctification of the Saints

When we come by faith to Christ, God transforms us into His new creation. Old things pass away, all things become new. One thing He does is to make the body of the believer His temple. Ephesians 2:21 speaks of us as being "an holy temple in the Lord." First Corinthians 3:17 tells us, "If any man defile the temple of God, him shall God destroy; for the temple of God is holy, which temple ye are." First Corinthians 6:19 and 20 say:

> What? know ye not that your body is the temple of the Holy [Spirit] which is in you, which ye have of God, and ye are not your own? For ye are bought with a price: therefore glorify God in your body, and in your spirit, which are God's.

Spurgeon refers to holiness as the architectural plan on which God builds up His living temple. First Corinthians 7:34 says we are "holy both in body and in spirit." We must recognize the need for sanctification or holiness within our lives if we are to please God.

Holiness is God's goal for every believer. Paul sets this forth clearly in Ephesians 1:4, "According as he hath chosen [or elected] us in him before the foundation of the world,

[Why?] that we should be holy and without blame before him in love." I once had a discussion with someone about the doctrine of election and noticed certain habits that he had not cleared up in his life. Although he was infatuated with the doctrine of election, he had missed the whole purpose of election: to be holy and without blame before God. God's goal for every believer is to be holy. The more we please God, the greater resemblance we will have to Him. We need to examine ourselves to see whether we look more like Jesus today than we did a year ago.

We are to pray with holiness in our lives, "lifting up holy hands" to Heaven in prayer (1 Tim. 2:8). If we regard iniquity in our hearts the Lord will not hear us. First Peter 2 gives several aspects of holiness in our lives. Verse 5 says we are a holy priesthood. "Ye also, as lively stones, are built up a spiritual house, an holy priesthood, to offer up spiritual sacrifices, acceptable to God by Jesus Christ." Our service must cultivate the fruit of goodness, because without it we fail to serve God properly. Verse 9 gives another aspect of goodness, "Ye are a chosen generation, a royal priesthood, an holy nation, a peculiar people; that ye should show forth the praises of him who hath called you out of darkness into his marvellous light." We must live as Heavenly citizens. God has set us apart for His special glory, and He glories in the holiness of His saints. Sam Lucas says, "The essence of true holiness consists in conformity to the nature and will of God."[1] Saints are to be "full of goodness, filled with all knowledge, able also to admonish one another" (Rom. 15:14). We cannot help other Christians until we have the fruit of goodness. Paul says we are able to admonish, minister to, build up and edify others because we are "full of goodness." Matthew Henry said, "Nothing can make a man truly great, but being truly good and partaking of God's holiness."[2] As we are filled with God's holiness, we can minister effectively to others.

III. The Outward Display of Holiness

The Bible commands us to be holy. Peter writes, "As he which hath called you is holy, so be ye holy in all manner of conversation; Because it is written, Be ye holy; for I am holy" (1 Pet. 1:15, 16). The question for us is, How do we practice the outward display of holiness? We must prove goodness. Romans 12:2 talks of knowing the will of God after we have presented our bodies a living sacrifice unto the the Lord and are transformed by the renewing of our minds. The end result is to prove that good, acceptable and perfect will of God.

An old Chinese proverb says there are two perfectly good men, one dead and the other unborn. I would like to add a third to that proverb. The other good person is the Christian who has surrendered his life to Christ. That person can prove the good will of God.

Once we know the good will of God, we must do it. Romans 12:9 speaks of cleaving to that which is good. The word "cleave" means "to be glued to it." We are to be glued to the goodness, righteousness and holiness of God. If we are stuck on goodness, we cannot change to nongoodness.

Romans 13:3 says, "Do that which is good." The context relates our action to those who rule over us. We are to be in submission to the authority over us: the child to the parents, the wife to her husband, the husband to God. Obedience is doing that which is good. Galatians 6:10 adds, ". . . let us do good unto all men, especially unto them who are of the household of faith." Goodness puts love into action by following the example of our Savior.

It requires hard work to cultivate goodness. Notice two examples in the book of Ephesians. First, "Let him that stole steal no more: but rather let him labour, working with his hands the thing which is good, that he may have to give to him that needeth" (Eph. 4:28). God wants to transform lives, not just provide an escape route from hell. Salvation is the transformation of one's whole character. The thief no longer steals but works with his hands so he can help others. Transformation is holiness put into action. The second example from Ephesians is, "Knowing that whatsoever good thing any man doeth, the same shall he receive of the Lord, whether he be bond or free" (Eph. 6:8). The employee is to serve his boss faithfully at all times, doing that which is good, in reality seeking to please the Lord. If you are having trouble with your boss at work, if he is mean or nasty to you, start asking God to help you do things that are good, seeking not just to please the boss but the Lord Jesus Christ. Paul talks of the works of goodness when he says, "But glory, honour, and peace, to every man that worketh good, . . ." (Rom. 2:10). Peace and goodness are interrelated; we cannot have one without the other. If we are to have inward peace, we must cultivate goodness.

In fact, the Bible commands us to follow after goodness. "See that none render evil for evil unto any man; but ever follow that which is good, both among yourselves, and to all men" (1 Thess. 5:15). Daniel Webster wrote, "Real goodness does not attach itself merely to this life, it points to another world. Political or professional reputation cannot last forever, but a conscience void of offence before God and man is an inheritance for eternity."[3] While the fame and reputation of some great hero fades away fast, goodness does not. The fruit of goodness will mark our lives for all eternity.

We are to be zealous for holiness. "It is good to be zealously affected always in a good thing, . . ." (Gal. 4:18). We had a plaque in our home authored by John Wesley which said, "Do all the good you can, in all the ways you can, to all the souls you can, at all the times you can, with all the zeal you can, as long as ever you can." That is zeal—goodness put into action.

Finally, we are to overcome evil with good. "Be not overcome of evil, but overcome evil with good" (Rom. 12:21). When the goodness of God is working within our lives, we are able to overcome evil, temptation, sin and anxiety. If something causes anxiety, God wants us to yield to His holiness so He can give us peace. When He is in control, we will glorify Him by zealously overcoming evil with good. Are you a good example of the fruit of the Spirit which is goodness? If so, remember:

Christ has no hands but our hands
To do His work today;
He has no feet but our feet
To lead men in His way;
He has no lips but our lips
To tell men how He died;
He has no help but our help
To bring them to His side.
We are the only Bible
The careless world will read;
We are the sinner's gospel;
We are the scoffer's creed;
We are our Lord's last message,
Written in word and deed.
(Annie Johnson Flint)

Research Bibliography

Bridge, Jerry. *The Pursuit of Holiness.* Colorado Springs: Navpress, 1978.
Culbertson, William. *God's Provision for Holy Living.* Chicago: Moody Press, 1968.
Gage, Robert. *The Birthmarks of the Christian Life* (chap. 3 and 7). Grand Rapids: Sword & Shield Ministries, 1978.
Murray, Andrew. *Holy in Christ.* New York: Randolf & Co., n.d.
Paxson, Ruth. *Called Unto Holiness.* Chicago: Moody Press, 1968.
Solomon, Charles. *Handbook to Happiness.* Wheaton, IL: Tyndale House, 1975.

Questions for Research and Discussion

1. How do gentleness and goodness relate to each other?
2. Study the holiness of God by using a concordance. Look up words like holiness, righteousness, perfectness and goodness.
3. While studying God's holiness (as above), note how God's Word requires the believer to be holy. Make a list of the expectations of God for the Christian's life.
4. Study 1 Peter 1:15, 16. Use the self-check list of those things in your life that do not conform to God's desires, and plan a solution for each one.

Sins of Omission

____ 1. Ingratitude toward God
____ 2. Lack of love toward God
____ 3. Neglect of Bible study
____ 4. Unbelief in God's Word
____ 5. Neglect of prayer
____ 6. No soul-winning desire
____ 7. Neglect of church
____ 8. Burying talents
____ 9. Neglect of family duties
____10. No tithing
____11. Unfaithfulness
____12. Procrastination
____13. Laziness and slothfulness
____14. Inhospitality

Sins of Commission

____ 1. Pride
____ 2. Judgmental attitude
____ 3. A bitter spirit toward another
____ 4. Envy
____ 5. Slander
____ 6. Lying and cheating
____ 7. Murmuring
____ 8. Hypocrisy
____ 9. Robbing God of time, ability, money
____10. Bad temper
____11. Profanity
____12. Overeating
____13. Speeding
____14. Improper dating relationships
____15. Immodesty

Sins of Omission

____15. Lack of "rejoicing always"
____16. Neglect of watching over your own life
____17. Neglect of watching over the brethren
____18. Failure of self-denial
____19. Lack of interest in missions
____20. Complacency

Sins of Commission

____16. Adultery
____17. Homosexuality
____18. Occult in-volvements
____19. Drugs
____20. Worldly-mindedness

5. As an experiment in humility, ask a close friend or relative to share with you areas of your life that need change and maturity. Do not argue with them but graciously accept their comments. Then, with God's help, take one item at a time and seek to change. Ask them a month later if they have noticed any improvement.

Chapter 10

The Fruit of the Spirit is

FAITH

A woman came to talk with an evangelist about her husband. She mentioned that her husband had been attending the evangelistic meetings and was glad he was enjoying them. "But," she added, "I'm wondering when he's going to stop singing 'Hold the Fort' and come home and hold the baby." She recognized the difference between what he was at church and what he was at home. Truly spiritual people are not only spiritual at church but are also spiritual at home, work or school. The key to being spiritual is in the word "faith," the Greek word meaning "faithfulness." The fruit of the Spirit is faithfulness.

I. Saving Faith

Saving faith brings us to acknowledge the truth of the gospel and receive Christ as Savior. Saving faith follows repentance. Jesus said in Mark 1:15, ". . . repent ye, and believe the gospel." This is faith in the finished work at Calvary for eternal life and the forgiveness of sin.

Saving faith comes from the heart, as Romans 10:9 and 10 say:

> That if thou shalt confess with thy mouth the Lord Jesus, and

> shalt believe in thine heart that God hath raised him from the dead, thou shalt be saved. For with the heart man believeth unto righteousness; and with the mouth confession is made unto salvation.

Paul talks of a heart faith as distinguished from head knowledge. Many people understand the message of the Bible with their minds without believing with their hearts. Heart faith is entrusting my eternal soul to Christ, believing He will save me from sin and give eternal life. Dr. Gardner Springs said, "Faith in Christ is not an exercise of the understanding merely; it is the affection of the heart. With the heart man believeth. To those who believe, Christ is precious."[1] Without this heart faith there will be no eternity with God in Heaven.

Saving faith is contrasted with works in Ephesians 2:8 and 9, "For by grace are ye saved through faith; and that not of yourselves: it is the gift of God: Not of works, lest any man should boast." No one is going to go around Heaven boasting, "I did this to get in here." God says the only boast anyone will have in Heaven is that Christ died to save sinners and that Christ saved him. That is the only boast we have—our boast in Christ and His finished work of redemption. He did that which we could not do. He satisfied all the righteous demands of God.

In my first church, a lady asked to have communion served at home. When I asked why, she answered, "I need it. I'm going to die." She was trusting the Lord's Table to get her to Heaven. If we trust works, church membership or baptism to get to Heaven, we will never get there. The only way to Heaven is through the Lord Jesus Christ and His finished work on the cross, which we trust by faith. The result is justification, as Romans 5:1 tells us, "Therefore being justified by faith, we have peace with God through our Lord Jesus Christ."

A young man, a caddy with the Women's P.G.A. tournament in White Plains, came to my study. He did not have Christ in his life. I asked him what he knew about the Bible and he told me everything that I could have told him. But when I asked, "What have you done about it?" he said, "Nothing." I then told him about the Lord Jesus Christ, and he received Christ as his personal Savior and was transformed into a new creation in Christ. Saving faith brought Christ into his life.

II. Living Faith

The Bible also talks about "living faith" in Hebrews chapter 11. The first three verses define living faith and the rest of the chapter gives many examples of it. "Faith is the substance of things hoped for, the evidence of things not seen. For by it the elders obtained a good report. Through faith we understand that the worlds were framed by the word of God, . . ." (vv. 1-3). "Without faith it is impossible to please him: for he that cometh to God must believe that he is . . ." (v. 6). Only a person who has experienced saving faith can realize a vital living faith.

This term "faith" found in Hebrews 11 is a firm conviction which produces the full acknowledgment of the Bible as God's revelation and message to us. In 2 Thessalonians 2:12 and 13 Paul illustrates it:

> That they all might be damned who believed not the truth, but had pleasure in unrighteousness. But we are bound to give thanks alway to God for you, brethren beloved of the Lord, because God hath from the beginning chosen you to salvation through sanctification of the Spirit and belief of the truth.

Those who do not believe the Bible come under the rightful judgment of a holy God. If a person does not believe the Bible is true, he will have a difficult time accepting the miracle of Christ's death on the cross of Calvary.

Not only is living faith a conviction of the truth, it is a personal surrender to the Lord. John 1:12 declares, "But as many as received him, to them gave he power [or authority] to become the sons of God, even to them that believe on his name." Faith is a surrender to the Person of the Son of God.

Rowland Hill once dealt with a lady regarding her salvation. She said she was a child of God because she dreamed "such and such a thing." He responded, "Never mind what you did while you were asleep, let's see what you will do while you are awake." Surrender to the Person of Christ is not some hazy, indefinite act. Dr. Horace Bushnell has said, "Faith is the act of trust by which a sinner commits himself to the Savior."[2] Be sure you have committed yourself to the Lord Jesus Christ for eternal salvation.

The result of such a surrender is described in 2 Corinthians 5:17, "Therefore if any man be in Christ, he is a new creature: old things are passed away; behold, all things are become new." This transformation in the believer's life causes him to live according to his beliefs. Hebrews chapter 11 shows people whose lives were changed because of their faith. This living, vital faith produced transformed lives that honored and glorified the Lord Jesus Christ.

Augustine said, "Faith is to believe what we do not see, and the reward of this faith is to see what we believe." This living faith must be cultivated in our lives as believers.

III. Walking Faith

Our living faith must become a walking faith. The fruit of the Spirit is faithfulness, that which God requires for every believer. First Corinthians 4:2 tells us, "Moreover it is required in stewards, that a man be found faithful." The Lord wants to reward the believer with the crowns He has promised in Scripture, but the basis of every reward is faithfulness. Stewards must be found faithful. It is not how much we have done but whether it was done in faithfulness. Whatever is not of faith is sin. If service is not done in faithfulness, the Lord cannot reward us. A pastor and his wife who had labored very successfully in many different fields of service were asked the reason for their success. Their response was, "We are always at our post." They were faithful. What is your post—a deacon, an usher? The Lord's question will not be whether you were a deacon or an usher, but whether you stood at your post faithfully. He will want to know if you served in faithfulness. Faithfulness is the key to rewards.

God offers His blessing upon faithfulness. The psalmist says, ". . . the LORD preserveth the faithful . . ." (Ps. 31:23). Have you ever been to that place in your life where everything seemed to be falling in on you? The Lord promises to preserve the faithful in those moments. We can look up to the Lord in faith and say, "I know You hold my hand, therefore I will walk with You today. I will not be afraid." When I was a little fellow, we were out for a drive in the old Willys. I was in the back seat looking out the window when the door flew open. There I was, holding onto the door, waving like a flag. Somehow my mother reached out and pulled me in. I am glad she had her hand on me.

God is like that to us. Faithfulness is putting ourselves in the hand of God. You may go through a trial this week, but God has His hand on you. Do not give up! Hang on and stay at your post. The Lord will bring deliverance. He knows our trials and He understands our problems. He knows the decisions we must make, the difficulties we face. He wants us to turn to Him and cultivate the fruit of faithfulness. Proverbs 13:17 says, ". . . a faithful ambassador is health." People who bring blessing into our lives are people who are faithful. They do their jobs right. They faithfully pray for us and display their love.

How important it is to have faithful prayer warriors. When we were visiting missionaries in South America, they all said their most important need was prayer. I thought of one of our shut-ins who, at ninety years of age, prayed four to six hours a day for missionaries. What a reward she will have for that faithfulness.

Proverbs 28:20 adds, "A faithful man shall abound

with blessings. . . ." If we want blessings in our lives, we must cultivate faithfulness to God.

God often rewards faithfulness with some new area of service. Look at what happened to Paul. In 1 Timothy 1:12, the apostle talks of his own experience, "I thank Christ Jesus our Lord, who hath enabled me, for that he counted me faithful, putting me into the ministry." After he was saved, Paul went to Jerusalem, where the people looked very skeptically at him. They were not sure he was a believer. So he went to Arabia for several years and studied the Scriptures faithfully. He was invited by Barnabas to minister in Antioch as an assistant pastor. He became a faithful Bible teacher. One day the Spirit of God said, "Separate Barnabas and Saul. I have a greater task for them." The reason God made him "Paul the apostle" was because he had been "Saul the faithful." Because he was faithful in the little things, God gave him something greater. You say, "God hasn't given me anything important to do in life." Then be faithful in doing what God asks you to do now. God will give you something else. He rewards faithfulness. Someone has said, "God has no larger field for the man who is not faithfully doing his work where he is." I remember reading a story about a boy who applied for a job in a hardware store. His first assignment was in the attic on the third floor. In the dirty, messy room was a big box full of old screws, nails, tools and junk. The manager dumped everything on the floor for the boy to sort and put in order within three days. Left alone, the young lad was tempted to take a nap because no one was watching him, but he determined to do faithfully as he had been asked. He put everything in order. When the manager saw what the boy had done he said, "Most people wouldn't do this job; but because you worked faithfully, I have a position for you, which will lead to a better position as you remain faithful." Faithfulness is doing what we have been asked to do. Doing our appointed task at the present time will bring new areas of service.

Faithfulness also brings eternal rewards. Concerning Christ's parable of the talents, Matthew 25:21 says, "His Lord said unto him, Well done, thou good and faithful servant: thou hast been faithful over a few things, I will make thee ruler over many things: enter thou into the joy of thy lord." We do not know what God has planned for us in eternity. We too often focus on what is happening now, when we should be laying up treasures in Heaven. Our faithfulness today is preparation for eternal service.

The crown of life is offered twice in the Bible; in James 1:12—"Blessed is the man that endureth temptation [or testing]: for when he is tried, he shall receive the crown of life, which the Lord hath promised to them that love him"—and in Revelation 2:10—"Fear none of those things which thou shalt suffer: behold, the devil shall cast some of you into prison, that ye may be tried; and ye shall have tribulation ten days: be thou faithful unto death, and I will give thee a crown of life." The crown of life is offered to believers who are faithful; to believers who trust the Lord during trials; to believers who still love the Lord during trials. It is offered to believers who are willing to die for the Lord during those trials. Faithfulness is God's final definition of a victorious life. Are we faithful in all things? Perry Tanksley wrote this about faithfulness:

> I saw you stand steadfast in grief
> But saw no trace of unbelief.
> I saw you stand unmoved by stress
> But saw no trace of bitterness.
> I saw you stand bravely for years
> But saw no trace of senseless fears.
> Though you spoke not of faith's firm law,
> I caught your faith by things I saw.[3]

Faith is contagious. When we believe God will fulfill the promises of His Word, others will believe it too. Our neighbors will see it. Fellows students will see it. Our friends, family and co-workers will see it. We must cultivate the fruit of faithfulness and make it evident in our lives.

Research Bibliography

Gage, Robert. *The Birthmarks of the Christian Life.* Grand Rapids: Sword & Shield Ministries, 1976.

Gordon, A. J. *In Christ.* Grand Rapids: Baker Book House, 1964.

Grubb, Norman. *The Law of Faith.* Ft. Washington, PA: Christian Literature Crusade, 1970.

Machen, J. Gresham. *What Is Faith?* Grand Rapids: Wm. B. Eerdmans Publishing Co., 1965.

Pierson, A. T. *George Mueller of Bristol.* Westwood, NJ: Fleming H. Revell Co., n.d.

Smith, Hannah W. *The Christian's Secret of a Happy Life.* Westwood, NJ: Fleming H. Revell Co., 1952.

Taylor, Howard. *Hudson Taylor's Spiritual Secrets.* Philadelphia: China Inland Mission, 1950.

Questions for Research

1. What is saving faith? Where does it come from and what is its result?
2. What is the relationship of Scripture to living faith?
3. How does surrender to Christ affect the life of a believer?
4. The fruit of faith is primarily "faithfulness." Make a list based on the Scriptures of areas of daily life where God requires faithfulness.
5. God offers rewards and blessings for faithfulness. Using the list you made above, what areas do you feel are acceptable to God in your life? What areas need improvement?

   a.

   b.

   c.

   d.

Chapter 11

The Fruit of the Spirit is

MEEKNESS

A Jamaican boy was asked by a missionary, "Who are the meek?" He responded, "Those that give soft answers to rough questions."

One of the more difficult aspects of the fruit of the Spirit that we are to cultivate is meekness. Meekness is a word meaning to be gentle, kind and not easily provoked. Meekness is humility in action. We could substitute the word humility for meekness, but it must be an active humility, involved in doing something.

When Dr. Morrison, the great missionary to China, was seeking an assistant, he instructed his secretary to examine the prospects carefully, telling her exactly what to say and do. One young man who came to be examined was Mr. Mills, later to be Dr. Mills, equal in fame and in scholarship with Morrison himself. After the interview, the secretary informed Mr. Mills that he was not fit or qualified to be an assistant to Dr. Morrison. "However," she added, "he is looking for a servant for his home. Would you be willing to take that position?" Mills replied, "I would gladly be a servant to this great man of God." Through his submission and humility, he was given the place as assistant to Dr. Morrison.

I. Biblical Examples of Meekness

Because there are so many wrong ideas about humility, let us look in the Bible for some examples. The first person described as being meek was Moses, in Numbers 12:3, ("Now the man Moses was very meek, above all the men which were upon the face of the earth."). We do not think of Moses as being meek when he struck the Red Sea with his rod and suddenly there was a roadway from Egypt to Sinai. Hear Moses defying Pharaoh as he says, "Let my people go!" Moses, meek? In the context of Number 12:3, Moses is choosing seventy people to be elders over Israel to serve with him. Miriam and Aaron had rebelled against Moses, but the context shows they were really rebelling against God. God, in proclaiming that Moses is meek, defends him and brings judgment upon those who rebelled.

The term "meek" is also given as a description of the nature of the Lord Jesus Christ. In 2 Corinthians 10:1 Paul says, "I . . . beseech you by the meekness and gentleness of Christ. . . ." Matthew's Gospel twice refers to Christ as being meek. His meekness is first revealed in Matthew 11:28 and 29: "Come unto me, all ye that labour and are heavy laden, and I will give you rest. Take my yoke upon you, and learn of me; for I am meek and lowly in heart: and ye shall find rest unto your souls." If meekness, or humility in action, were not part of the character of Jesus, He could not offer us rest and peace.

The humility of Christ is again seen in Matthew 21:5 as it tells of the triumphal entry of the Lord into Jerusalem, ". . . Behold, thy King cometh unto thee, meek. . . ." It is interesting that although Jesus is described as meek, He later overthrew the money changers and drove them out of the temple. Somewhere we got the wrong idea that meekness is equivalent to weakness. In the Bible, meekness is giving God the rightful place of leadership so that God, not the individual, is seen. Moses diminished himself to the point where God was in control of his life. The Lord Jesus Christ came to glorify the Father, Who was the central theme in His life so He could say, "If you have seen Me you have seen the Father."

The apostle Paul also put Christ first in his life. He asked the Corinthians, "What will ye? shall I come unto you with a rod, or in love, and in the spirit of meekness?" (1 Cor. 4:21). Paul saw two options in dealing with the church at Corinth: the rod of Scriptural discipline or instruction in love with meekness. Paul's meekness is seen in the description of 1 Corinthians 15:9 where he says he is the least of the apostles. Paul humbled himself before others.

Another group of people referred to as meek are mentioned in James 3. The person who is wise is meek. "Who is a wise man and endued with knowledge among you? let him show out of a good conversation [or a good way of living] his works with meekness of wisdom" (James 3:13). A wise person who puts the Word of God into practice will humble himself before God and seek to glorify God in all he does and thinks. When the Bible says the fruit of the Spirit is meekness, it refers to a person who allows Christ to control his life so the Holy Spirit can bring glory to God alone. The believer is diminished and Christ is lifted up. What a wonderful thing it would be if people would say when looking at our lives, "There goes a Christian. There goes someone who is glorifying the Lord." Instead of seeing us, they would see the Lord. This humility in action is the basis for true revival.

Someone has said, "Great men never feel great, small men never feel small. Great men make others feel great, small men make others feel small." Great people make others important. As they exercise the fruit of meekness, they seek to meet the needs of others and glorify God. Are we desirous of cultivating the fruit of meekness in our lives? In life we learn either humility or humiliation. If we allow pride to control our lives, the Lord will humble us. That is humiliation. If we put Christ in full charge of our lives, He will receive the glory. That is humility. The choice is ours.

II. The Blessings of Meekness

The Bible offers blessings for meekness. Zephaniah 2:3 commands, "Seek ye the Lord, all ye meek of the earth, which have wrought his judgment; seek righteousness, seek meekness: it may be ye shall be hid in the day of the Lord's anger." If we follow this command to seek meekness, several blessings are offered:

Psalm 22:26—The meek shall eat and be satisfied. . . .
Psalm 25:9—The meek will he guide in judgment; and the meek will he teach his way.
Psalm 37:11—The meek shall inherit the earth. . . .
Psalm 76:9—God arose to judgment, to save all the meek. . . .
Psalm 147:6—The LORD lifteth up the meek. . . .
Psalm 149:4—. . . he will beautify the meek with salvation.
Isaiah 29:19—The meek also shall increase their joy in the LORD. . . .

A wealthy businessman went to visit a small western college which was in financial trouble. He asked the gardener for directions to the president's house. The gardener pointed the direction but explained the president would not be there until noon. The man thanked the gardener and looked around the campus until noon. He knocked on the door of the college president's house and was surprised when the gardener opened the door. The man pulling the weeds out of the garden was the president. The businessman said, "Sir, I wasn't going to give a dime to your school, but if you are willing to humble yourself to care for the garden, you must have things going right." He wrote him a check for $50,000.

Now, we do not humble ourselves for money. There is something worth more than $50,000—the joy of the Holy Spirit. If we humble ourselves before Almighty God, He will bestow joy and other blessings upon us.

III. The Commands for Meekness

The believer is commanded to have a humble disposition before others.

Ephesians 4:1, 2—. . . walk worthy . . . With all lowliness and meekness. . . .
Colossians 3:12—Put on therefore, as the elect of God . . . meekness. . . .
1 Timothy 6:11—. . . O man of God . . . follow after . . . meekness.
Titus 3:2—. . . shewing all meekness unto all men.

Humility is also the key to effective witnessing. If we are to share the gospel with others, we must come with humility. First Peter 3:4 talks of a Christian woman who desires her unsaved husband to come to Jesus Christ as Savior. "But let it be the hidden man of the heart, in that which is not corruptible, even the ornament of a meek and quiet spirit, which is in the sight of God of great price." The woman who wears the disposition of meekness is going to more effectively bring her husband to Christ. She will be in subjection to her husband so that he may be won by the humble way in which she lives (1 Pet. 3:1). First Peter 3:15 adds, "But sanctify the Lord God in your hearts: and be ready always to give an answer to every man that asketh you a reason of the hope that is in you with meekness and fear." Our testimony must be presented in humility. We must recognize that we have no power to bring any person to Christ. Only the Spirit of God can be the soul winner and convict a lost sinner of his need and show him that Jesus Christ is the only way of salvation. As we recognize our dependency upon the Spirit of God, we will have the best results in witnessing. The Holy Spirit is looking for humble instruments He can use in winning lost people to Christ.

Humility is the key to effective Bible studying, preaching and teaching. James 1:21 reminds us, ". . . receive with meekness the engrafted word. . . ." We must humbly come to the Word of God and realize God has something to teach us.

I remember while in college attending a church that the students had nicknamed "the church of the frigid air." Students would bring their dictionaries so they could understand what was being said. I determined to try a different attitude. I prayed, "Lord, I need something today for my soul and you can use your servant to teach me." While others left frustrated, I went out blessed because I had opened my heart and mind to the Spirit of God. He can use anybody to teach us if we let Him. We must humble ourselves before God and allow the Scriptures to saturate our lives.

In preaching the Word of God there must be humility. Isaiah 61:1 says, ". . . the LORD hath anointed me to preach good tidings unto the meek. . . ." Not only must the preacher hide himself behind Calvary, but he must recognize that the reception of the Word of God depends upon the people humbling themselves before God. If the listener recognizes his needs and humbles himself before God, God will meet those needs. If we go to church demanding, "What have you got for me?" we probably will go out as empty as we came in. Only as we humble ourselves before God can He teach us.

Spiritual correction and teaching are also to be done with meekness. Paul says in 2 Timothy 2:24–26:

> And the servant of the Lord must not strive; but be gentle unto all men, apt to each, patient, In meekness instructing those that oppose themselves; if God peradventure will give them repentance to the acknowledging of the truth; And that they may recover themselves out of the snare of the devil, who are taken captive by him at his will.

If we wish to teach people who are walking in error, we cannot deal with them arrogantly. We may win the argument because we have the Word of God but lose people doing it. We need to instruct with meekness from the Scripture so they can see the error of their way. H. W. Webb-Peploe once said, "What God wants is men great enough, to be small enough, to be used."[1] When Charles Brontë was dying he was too proud to call a doctor and even too proud to lie down. He died standing up. Too many Christians are the same way. Others are like the man who prayed, "Lord, make me a doormat." When God made that person a doormat and he was trampled upon by others, he complained and manifested an opposite spirit from his prayer.

On the other hand is Moses who humbled himself before God, admitting there were better people to do the job. He was a poor speaker, but the Lord had him speak before the king of Egypt. Perhaps the Lord wants you to sing in the choir, be an usher, teach a class, go to the mission field or preach. God wants men who are great enough to be small enough to be used. Will you humble yourself and ask the Lord to use you? "He hath shewed thee, O man, what is good; and what doth the LORD require of thee, but to do justly, and to love mercy, and to walk humbly with thy God?" (Micah 6:8). When that verse is fulfilled in our lives, we will be filled with the fruit of the Spirit which is meekness, or humility in action. God is looking for someone who will humble himself to be used for His glory.

Here are a few suggestions for cultivating humility in our lives:

- Spend time daily in the Scriptures. Read them. Study them. Meditate upon them. Memorize a verse a day.
- Daily submit your life to God's control and influence. Do this the first thing each morning and remind yourself of it several times throughout the day.
- Pray for others. Become conscious of their needs and burdens. Put your prayers into action by being willing to help bear their burdens.
- Put others first, your own plans and ambitions second. Avoid the pitfalls of selfishness and self-interests. Listen to others—do not do all the talking. Be genuinely concerned. Pray with them.

- Consciously test every thought and motive. Bring them into obedience to Christ. Learn to think and act Biblically.
- Be slow in taking offense. Be quick in acknowledging faults in your life that have offended others. Daily examine your life and confess any sin to God. If needed, seek the forgiveness of others.
- Learn to compliment others. Build them up, do not tear them down. Avoid gossip and negative, destructive criticism. Seek to praise the good points of others.
- Be willing to accept persecution and trials with joy and long-suffering. Avoid retaliation. Be quick to forgive and overlook the faults of others.

Remember, meekness is humility in action. As soon as we think we have arrived at humility, we lose it. This aspect of spiritual fruit must continually be cultivated in our lives. When properly done, others will know it and God will bless it. Keep cultivating.

Research Bibliography

Bernard de Clairvaux. *The Steps of Humility*. Translated by Geoffrey Webb. London: A. R. Morbray, 1957.

Marsh, F. E. *The Spiritual Life*. London: Pickering and Inglis, n.d.

Murray, Andrew. *Humility, the Beauty of Holiness*. Westwood, NJ: Fleming H. Revell, n.d.

Rossays, James E. *Abiding in Christ*. Grand Rapids: Zondervan, 1973.

Thomas à Kempis. *Imitation of Christ*. London: J. M. Dent, 1910.

Thomas, Ian. *The Mystery of Godliness*. Grand Rapids: Zondervan, 1964.

Questions for Research and Discussion

1. Study the examples of meekness. Why is meekness *not* weakness?

2. What benefits does one receive from being humble?

 a.

 b.

 c.

 d.

 e.

3. How can you tell if someone is humble? Make a list of examples of humility you see in the lives of other Christians or people in the Bible.

	Examples of humility	How can I follow this example?
a.		
b.		
c.		
d.		
e.		

4. How does a humble disposition affect our witnessing?

5. How does a humble disposition affect our study and use of the Scriptures?

Chapter 12

The Fruit of the Spirit is

SELF-CONTROL

The real evidence of true spiritual maturity is acting and thinking Biblically by cultivating the fruit of the Spirit which is love, joy, peace, longsuffering, gentleness, goodness, faith, meekness and temperance. Temperance is a Greek word meaning strength. Its English form means self-control. The Latin word means moral courage, speaking of a person who has the strength of self-control. Self-control is like a lever within man's personality that God uses to stop his runaway spirit. Self-control is promoted by humility. Someone has wisely said, "He who rules himself is the greatest of monarchs."

I. Self-Control of the Body

Self-control relates to the body. First Corinthians 9:25 says, "Every man that striveth for the mastery is temperate. . . ." Self-control of the body is the theme of Paul at the end of this chapter. Follow the illustration of a marathon runner:

> Know ye not that they which run in a race run all, but one receiveth the prize? So run, that ye may obtain. And every man that striveth for the mastery is temperate in all things. Now they do it to obtain a corruptible crown; but we an incorruptible. I therefore so run, not as uncertainly; so fight I, not as one that

> beateth the air: But I keep under my body, and bring it into subjection: lest that by any means, when I have preached to others, I myself should be a castaway (1 Cor. 9:24–27).

Many people are crowded together at the starting line of the marathon race. As the pistol smoke appears, off they go. Twenty-six miles later they are headed toward the finish, but only one person will get the prize.

Paul is saying that the person who comes in first will be the one who controls his body. He puts everything physically into running that race. He is not thinking of a steak dinner later in the evening, nor is he worrying about his sore feet. He is thinking about keeping his body functioning properly, using every ounce of strength to reach the finish line. This runner is a successful runner.

Paul then says, "So run that ye may obtain." Spiritually we are in a race. To win, our bodies must be controlled by our souls. Self-control means mastery. "Every man that striveth for the mastery is [self-controlled]." The person who cultivates this aspect of the fruit of the Spirit does so because he wants to be the very best he can be for God. He will not settle for second best. He will work according to his best ability and talents. He will improve himself as God gives the capability. He commands himself. His soul directs his body. If his body dictated to his soul, he might get hungry and decide to stop. Those who do not control their bodies might allow the pain in their legs or ankles to stop them. If a runner is to win the race, his soul will command his aching legs to keep going to the goal and to victory.

Pythagoras set down the rule that, "No man is free who cannot command himself." Freedom in Christ comes from the Spirit of God living and abiding in us. To have true freedom, we must cultivate the fruit of self-control, or the mastery of self. Our reward is an incorruptible crown, not some trophy that collects dust in the corner of a closet. The trophies and heroes of yesterday are soon forgotten, but self-controlled believers have an eternal reward. The incorruptible crown will never fade or be forgotten.

Self-control leads to self-discipline, making us sure of ourselves. Paul says, "I therefore so run, not as uncertainly." He knew the goals God had for him. In a marathon race there will be only one person to receive the crown, but in the spiritual life every Christian can receive the incorruptible crown. That is so because the goals or finish line God has for your life will be different from those for everyone else. God is looking for self-controlled faithfulness in our lives. We are to finish the task and fulfill the desires He has for us. The result is the incorruptible crown. A good marathon runner runs with self-discipline and becomes confident of himself. Many people lose self-confidence because they lose control emotionally, mentally or spiritually. Whenever people are undisciplined, ungodliness abounds. Lack of spiritual discipline in personal devotions and in prayer causes things to go wrong in our lives.

Self-control primarily relates to the body in 1 Corinthians 9:27, "But I keep under my body, and bring it into subjection: lest that by any means, when I have preached to others, I myself should be a castaway." One evangelist, after preaching, would go to his room where no one could interrupt him. There he would lie on the floor looking Heavenward and ask God to humble him so Christ could get the glory from the results that had been experienced that night. He would recite the words, "I bring my body under subjection lest when I preach to others I myself should be a castaway." Often our flesh runs away in pride when some great spiritual success has been achieved. We soon end up straggling behind in defeat.

We need to bring the body into subjection because it is the temple of the Holy Spirit.

> What? know ye not that your body is the temple of the Holy [Spirit] which is in you, which ye have of God, and ye are not

> your own? For ye are bought with a price: therefore glorify God in your body, and in your spirit, which are God's (1 Cor. 6:19, 20).

If the body is the temple, then the soul is the priest of the temple and should control the temple. Therefore, the soul should govern what the body does. When the body is tempted by the lust of the flesh, the lust of the eyes and the pride of life, the soul must say no! That is self-control. That body is disciplined by the soul to glorify God in all its actions.

The body should be governed by the soul in what it eats. Since the body is the temple of the Holy Spirit, we should govern what we eat, relating that to the care of the body. If a person is twenty pounds overweight on the insurance chart, he may be sinning against his body because it belongs to the Spirit of God. We must discipline our bodies so they will glorify the Holy Spirit.

We must also govern the cleanliness and appearance of our bodies. When an old Scottish preacher walked to the back of the church, a lady walked up to him and sniffed him, saying, "Sir, you use perfume." He turned, sniffed her back and said, "Ma'am, you don't!" We should be sure our bodies glorify God before others, thereby furthering our witness.

Finally, we should also govern how our bodies perform. Remember the Bible says that bodily exercise profits a little. We need not be obsessed with physical exercise, but we should get some. The body should be kept in tune so that God can use it as an instrument to glorify Christ. Do not cut your life short by neglect of your body.

II. Self-Control of the Will and Mind

The soul must also control the will and mind. We are to cultivate self-control over the will so our decisions will glorify the Lord. Paul, when talking to Felix, "reasoned of righteousness, temperance [or self-control], and judgment to come" (Acts 24:25). Felix, trembling, answered, "Go thy way for this time; when I have a convenient season, I will call for thee" (Acts 24:25). Notice the three areas Paul zeroed in on as he dealt with this man's spiritual life.

The first is righteousness. This is the righteousness of the Lord Jesus Christ as the only source of salvation. The Bible says, ". . . There is none righteous, no, not one." All mankind are sinners in the sight of God, for all have sinned and come short of His glory. But Jesus Christ, God's only Son, born of a virgin, incarnate of the Holy Spirit, lived a sinless life because He was the righteous Son of God. Paul was presenting the fact that Christ alone can satisfy the righteous demands of God.

The second is judgment. The "judgment to come" refers to the fact that the unsaved must stand at the Great White Throne Judgment before God. While many will boast of their own righteousness, they will be reminded that salvation is not by works of righteousness which we have done, but according to His mercy. Unless we come to the grace of Christ, judgment is certain.

The third is temperance. Temperance in this context relates to the sinner's repentance and faith in Christ. It is his spiritual surrender to God, admitting that God's Word is true and appropriating Christ by faith. Self-control in repentance and faith requires decisions of the will. The soul is requiring the will to be obedient to the Scriptures.

There must also be self-control over the mind. In 2 Peter 1:5–10, Peter gives a list of eight characteristics of the divine nature at work in the believer's life. His formula is:

> Faith + Virtue + Knowledge + Self-Control + Patience + Godliness + Kindness + Love = Fruitfulness + Spiritual Insight + Stability

Notice self-control is right in the middle. If we have knowledge without virtue we will be arrogant. We must first deal with our character, then add wisdom. Many people do the opposite; they have knowledge but no virtue. That is the folly of secular humanism—knowledge with no moral character or truth. Knowledge must have self-control. The soul must bring every thought into captivity to the obedience of Christ.

Each of us needs to consider how well he controls his thought life. To clean up our minds, we need self-control over our minds, which will build up the character of Christ in us.

III. Control of Self by the Spirit

So far we have said that the soul must control the body, the will and the mind. Self-control also involves one further step.

In Galatians 5:25 we read, "If we live in the Spirit, let us also walk in the Spirit." There needs to be control of the soul by the Spirit of God. When my soul is surrendered to the Holy Spirit, my soul can deal with my body, will and mind, making them obedient to Jesus Christ.

If the Holy Spirit is not in control of my soul, I will have great problems. Paul says we need to be living and walking in the Spirit. Living in the Spirit deals with the enjoyment of the Spirit's life through cultivating the fruit of the Spirit. One requirement for living in the Spirit is to crucify the flesh. "And they that are Christ's have crucified the flesh with the affections and lusts" (Gal. 5:24). Living in the Spirit results from the crucifixion of the affections and lusts of the flesh. Self-control of affections deals with our passions. Self-control of lusts deals with our selfish desires. When we put them in their place through temperance, we defeat them and gain victory through the Spirit of God. We cultivate self-mastery by yielding ourselves to the one great Master. We must turn our lives over to the control of the Spirit in order to walk in the Spirit. Walking in the Spirit results in our pride being placed aside for the glory of Christ. "But God forbid that I should glory, save in the cross of our Lord Jesus Christ, by whom the world is crucified unto me, and I unto the world" (Gal. 6:14). Surrender to Christ places God in full control. The final step in the cultivation of the fruit of self-control is making Christ Lord and Master.

Research Bibliography

Adams, Jay. *How to Overcome Evil.* Grand Rapids: Baker Book House, 1977.

Hyder, O. Quentin. *Shape Up.* Old Tappan, NJ: Fleming H. Revell, 1979.

LaHaye, Tim. *Spirit-Controlled Temperament.* Wheaton, IL: Tyndale House, 1974.

LeTourneau, Richard. *Keeping Your Cool in a World of Tension.* Grand Rapids: Zondervan, 1975.

Pierson, A. T. *Godly Self-Control.* Barkingside, Essex, Eng.: G. F. Vallance, n.d.

Sanders, John Oswald. *The Pursuit of the Holy.* Grand Rapids: Zondervan, 1976.

Strombeck, John. *Disciplined by Grace.* Chicago: Moody Press, 1946.

Questions for Research and Discussion

1. Make a list of areas where self-control over the body is necessary.
2. Use the following chart to show the use of self-control in the soul.

How can I control (by self-control)?

Mind	Will	Emotions
1.	1.	1.
2.	2.	2.
3.	3.	3.
4.	4.	4.

3. What is the purpose of self-control?
4. How does the Holy Spirit effect self-control in the life of the believer?
5. List areas where you need self-control and show your plan to achieve it.

Area where self-control is needed	How I plan to achieve self-control
1.	
2.	
3.	
4.	

Chapter 13

Walking in the Spirit

A man saw a workman pushing a wheelbarrow over a rough piece of ground and asked what he was doing. The workman replied, "I'm making a garden." The naive city slicker responded in surprise, "I thought gardens just grew." It takes many weeks of backbreaking toil before a garden will produce anything. Likewise, the fruit of the Spirit does not just happen. It often takes backbreaking toil to cultivate our souls, minds and hearts in developing love, joy, peace, longsuffering, gentleness, goodness, faith, meekness and self-control. As someone wisely said, "No man becomes a saint in his sleep."

Galatians 5:25 commands, "If we live in the Spirit, let us also walk in the Spirit." Walking in the Spirit is in reality letting the fruit of the Spirit be seen in our lives. Consider three practical steps for developing a spiritual walk.

I. Be Spiritually Filled Daily

To have a spiritual walk we must be filled by the Spirit of God every day. When we are saved, we are indwelt by the Spirit once for all. But there also comes a time of spiritual surrender when we allow the Spirit of God to take over our lives. The filling of the Spirit is defined in Ephesians 5:18, "Be not drunk with wine, wherein is excess; but be filled with the Spirit." The Greek tense means to be filled continually. Unlike the indwelling of the Spirit, it is not a once-for-all event, but a daily affair. The filling of the Spirit is related to power for special service, endurance of trials and dealings with problems. These situations in life demand that we be filled by the Spirit of God. Filling produces the spiritual fruit and becomes the basis of our daily walk in the Spirit.

There are three necessary steps for being filled daily. The first step is to daily confess known sins to God. "If we confess our sins, he is faithful and just to forgive us our sins, and to cleanse us from all unrighteousness" (1 John 1:9). "If I regard iniquity in my heart, the Lord will not hear me" (Ps. 66:18). Too many Christians are in the habit of waiting to confess their sins at the end of the day. Then they cannot remember them. As soon as we realize we have disobeyed the Scriptures and grieved the Spirit, we should confess our sin.

The second step is a complete submission or surrender of our bodies to the Lord. In Romans 6:11 through 13 Paul writes:

> Likewise reckon ye also yourselves to be dead indeed unto sin, but alive unto God through Jesus Christ our Lord. Let not sin therefore reign in your mortal body, that ye should obey it in the lusts thereof. Neither yield ye your members as instruments of unrighteousness unto sin: but yield yourselves unto God, as those that are alive from the dead, and your members as instruments of righteousness unto God.

The believer is to have victory through the filling of the Spirit in his life. Reckoning yourself to be dead to sin and alive to God is a step of faith. The Word of God assures us that our old natures died when Christ died on Calvary. The new natures are made alive to God by the power of Christ's resurrection. Faith in this fact means that sin is not allowed to reign in our bodies. By faith we yield our hands, feet, eyes and ears as instruments of righteousness for God. This spiritual surrender is described in Romans 12:1, "I beseech you therefore, brethren, by the mercies of God, that ye present [once for all] your bodies a living sacrifice, holy, acceptable unto God. . . ." Then daily we bring the members of our bodies into subjection to Christ.

The third factor in being filled with the Spirit daily is to commit ourselves to the control of the Holy Spirit and thank Him for it. In Luke 11:13 Jesus said to His disciples, "If ye then, being evil, know how to give good gifts unto your children: how much more shall your heavenly Father give the Holy Spirit to them that ask him?" When I was born again, the Spirit of God came into my life. Now He desires to bring victory to my life. Therefore, I must in prayer ask Him for that victory and claim the power of the Spirit.

An old farmer gave the same testimony at every prayer meeting: "I'm not making much progress, but I am established." One day this farmer was hauling some logs with his tractor when it got stuck in the mud. A neighbor, who attended the same prayer meetings, came by and said, "I see you're not making much progress, but you sure are established." If we are not making much progress in our Christian lives, we will miss what it means to be filled with the Spirit of God. We are just stuck in the mud and not getting anywhere. Progress is needed in our spiritual development. Peter prayed that we would grow in grace. Someone has suggested if we do not grow in grace we will groan in disgrace.

II. Be Sensitive to Sin

If we are to walk in the Spirit we need to be sensitive to sin. There are two passages of Scripture that are of vital importance to being sensitive to sin. One talks about grieving the Holy Spirit, the other quenching the Holy Spirit. Ephesians 4:30- 32 says:

> And grieve not the holy Spirit of God, whereby ye are sealed

> unto the day of redemption. Let all bitterness, and wrath, and anger, and clamour, and evil speaking, be put away from you, with all malice: And be ye kind one to another, tenderhearted, forgiving one another, even as God for Christ's sake hath forgiven you.

This passage of Scripture lists six sins of hostility toward other people that grieve the Holy Spirit. These sins of improper communication will disrupt our spiritual walk.

Bitterness	The Greek word means "to cut" and has the idea of a pointed, bitter hatred, usually the result of a lack of forgiveness or thankfulness. Unthankfulness and resentment will produce a bitter spirit.
Wrath	The word means "hot anger," expressing the idea of a passionate outburst. This is reacting to others by blowing our stack.
Anger	Anger has a view of taking revenge. It is an internal wrath that says, "I don't get mad, I get even."
Clamor	Clamor is an outcry that produces a turmoil of controversy. Some people love to argue just to cause problems and get attention. This clamor results in disunity and dissension among believers.
Evil Speaking	Blasphemy is tearing down someone else's character or judging a person's motives. Evil speaking is a disastrous sin along with the sin of gossip.
Malice	Malice means to be bad in quality, to be vicious. Malice is a combination of bitterness and anger. Bitter hatred produces revenge.

These things need to be guarded against in our lives. We must replace our corrupt way of life by being renewed in the spirit of our minds (Eph. 4:22–24). Begin appropriating Biblical truths and principles which will edify and minister grace unto the hearers (v. 29). In our relationships with other people, we must avoid these six sins of hostility or they will destroy the power of the Spirit of God.

We also need to be sensitive to quenching the Spirit through fear and worry. Most of the things we fear or worry about never happen. Fear and worry will destroy us if we do not surrender ourselves to the Spirit. First Thessalonians 5:19 says, "Quench not the Spirit." The context of this verse lists ten wrong attitudes that will quench the Holy Spirit.

1. A wrong attitude toward pastors (vv. 12, 13)

Not recognizing their spiritual admonition and refusing to esteem them highly in love is a sin. Any time we reject God's leadership we reject God Himself and His rule in our lives. Such a rejection of leadership has quenched the power of the Spirit of God in many churches across our land.

2. A wrong attitude toward other church members (v. 13)

We are to be at peace among ourselves. An unsubmissive spirit that breaks the unity of believers will quench the power of the Spirit. That is why the psalmist says it is good for brethren to dwell together in unity (Ps. 133:1).

3. A lack of church discipline and burden bearing (v. 14)

We are commanded to use church discipline to warn those who walk unruly. We are also to comfort the feebleminded, or the weak and despondent, who have little faith. We are to support the weak. Paul tells us to bear one another's burdens and so fulfill the law of Christ. We must have patience toward all, remembering that God is not finished with us yet.

4. Retaliation (v. 15)

Rendering evil for evil rather than doing that which is good is a spirit of retaliation or revenge which will quench the power of the Spirit.

5. A lack of rejoicing (v. 16)

"Rejoice evermore" turned around means quenching the power of the Spirit by lack of joy. Mumbling and grumbling are results of negative heart attitudes.

6. A lack of prayer (v. 17)

A lack of praying without ceasing produces unfaithfulness, which will turn off the power of the Spirit.

7. A lack of thanksgiving (v. 18)

Giving thanks in everything is the will of God for all believers. Remember, an unthankful attitude results in bitterness. We need to be thankful in every area of our lives.

8. Despising of preaching (v. 20)

We are to give careful attention to the preaching of the Word of God through His ministers. Despising the Word will quench spiritual power.

9. A careless attitude toward good doctrine (v. 21)

We are to prove good doctrine by putting it into practice in our lives. What God shows us He requires of us. Doctrine is to be proven experientially in our lives.

10. A careless attitude toward separation from worldliness (v. 22)

We are to avoid even the appearance of evil. If my "liberty" offends a weaker brother and causes him to sin against the Lord, I have misused it and the power of the Spirit will be quenched.

III. Be Scripturally Oriented

To walk in the Spirit also means to be Scripturally oriented. Tim LaHaye says the reading and study of the Bible helps us in the following ways:

It makes our way prosperous and gives success (Josh. 1:8).
It produces fruitfulness (Ps. 1:3).
It keeps us from sin (Ps. 119:11).

God reveals Himself to those who keep His word (John 14:21).
It cleanses us (John 15:3).
It produces power in prayer (John 15:7).
It brings joy to our hearts (John 15:11).
It gives victory over the wicked one (1 John 2:13, 14).[1]

The Bible commands the development of Biblical thinking in Romans 12:2, "And be not conformed to this world: but be ye transformed by the renewing of your mind, that ye may prove what is that good, and acceptable, and perfect, will of God." As we allow God's Word to control our minds, we will develop a new thinking process. This renewing of our minds enables us to prove what is good and acceptable and perfect in God's sight.

An old Irish farmer who had recently lost his eyesight was confronted one day on the street by a friend, who said, "I feel so bad for you; you must be very despondent over the loss of your eyesight." The Irishman answered, "I certainly am not! I just praise God for the years He gave me sight to enjoy all the wonderful things He has created." That is a different way of thinking than most people have regarding their problems and difficulties. An unknown poet expressed it this way:

O let my trembling soul be still,
And wait Thy wise, Thy holy will!
I cannot, Lord, Thy purpose see,
Yet all is well since ruled by Thee.

The person who is walking in the Spirit recognizes God is in control of everything in his life. Problems do not cause worry and fear. He has the Holy Spirit to walk with him through the problem. The Spirit goes with him through the valley of the shadow of death, so there is no fear. Tragedy does not cause anxiety. God holds him in His everlasting arms.

If he walks in the flesh, he has every reason for anxiety, fear and worry for he quenches and grieves the Holy Spirit. Then His power is turned off and the individual becomes an ineffective Christian. He becomes unsuccessful in living the Christian life, and there is no display of the fruit of the Spirit.

Thank God for the Holy Spirit Who indwells us and cares for us. We can have victory only as we walk in the Spirit and cultivate the fruit of the Spirit which is:

Love

Joy

Peace

Longsuffering

Gentleness

Goodness

Faith

Meekness

and

Self-Control

Research Bibliography

Bonar, Horatius. *God's Way of Holiness.* Chicago: Moody Press, n.d.

Briscoe, D. Stuart. *Living Dangerously.* Grand Rapids: Zondervan, 1972.

Ketcham, Robert T. *God's Provision for Normal Christian Living.* Chicago: Moody Press, 1963.

LaHaye, Tim. *Transformed Temperaments.* Wheaton, IL: Tyndale House, 1972.

McConkey, James. *The Three-fold Secret of the Holy Spirit.* Pittsburgh: Silver Publishing Society, 1897.

Mundell, George H. *The Ministry of the Holy Spirit.* Darby, PA: Maranatha Publications, n.d.

Nee, Watchman, *The Release of the Spirit.* Cloverdale, IN: Sure Foundation, 1965.

Questions for Research and Discussion

1. What is the difference between the indwelling and the filling of the Holy Spirit? How often do we need to be indwelt? How often do we need to be filled?
2. Use the following checklist to determine if you are prepared for spiritual filling.

   ☐ All known sins confessed
   ☐ Body surrendered to God
   ☐ Committed my life to the Holy Spirit's control
   ☐ Seeking to control my thoughts by the Scripture
   ☐ Seeking to make Biblically based decisions
   ☐ Seeking to have Biblically oriented behavior
3. Make a list of things you can do to make your actions and thinking Scripturally oriented.
4. In Ephesians 4:10–32 there is a list of wrong communications that grieve the Holy Spirit. Use the following chart as a self-check list to make sure you are not grieving the Holy Spirit.

Corrupt communication that grieves the Spirit

☐ Bitterness	☐ Clamor
☐ Wrath	☐ Evil Speaking
☐ Anger	☐ Malice

5. In 1 Thessalonians 5:12–22 there are a number of things mentioned that quench the power of the Holy Spirit. Use this self-check list to discover anything that is quenching the Spirit in your life.

Wrong attitudes that quench the Spirit

- ☐ Wrong attitudes toward pastors
- ☐ Wrong attitudes toward other church members
- ☐ Lack of church discipline and burden bearing
- ☐ Retaliation
- ☐ Lack of rejoicing
- ☐ Lack of thanksgiving
- ☐ Despising of preaching
- ☐ Careless attitude toward good doctrine
- ☐ Careless attitude toward separation
- ☐ Lack of prayer

Notes

Chapter two

1. S. D. Gordon, *Quiet Talks on Prayer* (New York: Fleming H. Revell, 1903), 44.

Chapter five

1. Wendell P. Loveless, *New Sunrise Meditations* (Grand Rapids: Eerdmans Publishing Co., 1942), 16, 17.

Chapter seven

1. W. E. Vine, *An Expository Dictionary of New Testament Words,* vol. 3 (Westwood, NJ: Fleming H. Revell, 1940), 12.

Chapter eight

1. Tyron Edwards, *The New Dictionary of Thoughts* (New York: Standard Book Co., 1963), 232.
2. Ibid.
3. Tyron Edwards, *Useful Quotations* (New York: Britikin Publishing Co., 1927), 202.
4. Ibid.

Chapter nine

1. Edwards, *Useful Quotations,* 258.
2. Ibid., 235.
3. Edwards, *Dictionary of Thoughts,* 239.

Chapter ten

1. G. B. Hallock, *5000 Best Modern Illustrations* (New York: Richard Smith, Inc., 1931), 264.
2. Ibid.
3. Perry Tanksley, *These Things I've Loved* (Jackson, MS: Allgood Books, 1971), 122. Attempt to obtain permission failed.

Chapter eleven

1. Hallock, *Modern Illustrations,* 378.

Chapter thirteen

1. Tim LaHaye, *Transformed Temperaments* (Wheaton, IL: Tyndale House, 1971), 141.

Bibliography

Edwards, Tyron. *The New Dictionary of Thoughts.* New York: Standard Book Co., 1963.

————————. *Useful Quotations.* New York: Britikin Publishing Co., 1927.

Gordon, S. D. *Quiet Talks on Prayer.* New York: Fleming H. Revell, 1903.

Hallock, G. B. *5000 Best Modern Illustrations.* New York: Richard Smith, Inc., 1931.

LaHaye, Tim. *Transformed Temperaments.* Wheaton, IL: Tyndale House, 1971.

Loveless, Wendell P. *New Sunrise Meditations.* Grand Rapids: Eerdmans Publishing Co., 1942.

Tanksley, Perry. *These Things I've Loved.* Jackson, MS: Allgood Books, 1971.

Vine, W. E. *An Expository Dictionary of New Testament Words.* Vol. 3. Westwood, NJ: Fleming H. Revell, 1940.